PREPARING IS ESSENTIAL

PREPARING YOURSELF FOR A JOB INTERVIEW

to get your dream job!

Allan Rufus

Copyright © 2015 Allan Rufus

PREPARING YOURSELF FOR A JOB INTERVIEW

First printing April 2015

http://allanrufus.org/my-published-books

coachingyoutosuccess@gmail.com

ISBN-13:
978-1500184988

ISBN-10:
1500184985

PERSONAL DEVELOPMENT TOOLS

DEDICATED TO YOU

"BEFORE ANYTHING ELSE,
PREPARATION IS KEY TO SUCCESS!"
- Alexander Graham Bell

"IF YOU FAIL TO PREPARE,
YOU'RE PREPARED TO FAIL"!
– Mark Spitz

CONTENTS

1   INTRODUCTION   1

2   PART 1 - HOME PREPARATIONS   5

- Deciding what you want to do

- Common Mistakes

- Knowing your skills, talents, qualities and traits

- Job searching

- Application process

- Things to think about when creating your CV / Resume

- Creating your CV / Resume

- Know your CV / Resume backwards

- Writing a cover letter

- Getting directions

- Researching the company

- What to take with you

- Getting groomed

- What to wear

- Prepare Mentally

- Social media sites

3   PART 2 - AT THE INTERVIEW   37

- What to expect

- What to remember while in the interview

- Business Etiquette

- First Impressions

- Body Language

- Greetings

- How to have a good interview

- Understand the interviewers agenda

- Branding yourself / Selling your skills

- What questions are most asked

- What questions to ask

- What questions not to ask

- How to negotiate your salary

- What questions to ask after the offer

- When you should NOT take the job

- Responsibilities

4   PART 3 - AFTER THE INTERVIEW   64

- Write down notes about the interview for future reference

- Write a thank you note

- Follow up

5   A CHECK LIST TO TAKE WITH YOU   68

6   TEMPLATES   72

- Cover Letter

- Resume

- Thank-you Letter

7   WORKBOOK – SKILLS IDENTIFICATION   84
AND GOAL SETTING

- Life's satisfaction scorecard - Page 90

Discovering your genius: Understanding yourself
and identifying your Core Beliefs:

- IQ vs EQ   Page 96

- Attitude   Page 99

- Self talk   Page 103

- Values   Page 107

- Desires   Page 114

- Qualities / Traits   Page 116

- Talents   Page 128

- Skills   Page 130

- Strengths   Page 143

- Weakness   Page 145

- Passion - Hobbies / Abilities   Page 151

- Goals   Page 156

8   CONCLUSION   Page 178

INTRODUCTION

*"Life is a step–by–step process, and each step matters,
so watch where you put your foot!" - Allan Rufus*

You need to be prepared physically and mentally by having a clear, practical and concise step-by-step strategy or roadmap when going for your job interview. You want to be relaxed, sound and look confident. You want to impress the interviewer with your presentation skills so you can be that outstanding candidate they are looking for.

I trust this book will give you a valuable understanding about what is needed and how to go about the job interview process. Use it as a guide to give you a direction to go in like a map would. When you have a map, your journey becomes a lot easier and more pleasant when you know where you are going, although it can also be fun and an adventure in itself if you choose to go by trial and error, however, it is not always the best option!

This book has two sections to it. Section 1 is all about the job interview process: Home preparations; At the Interview and After the Interview. Section 2 is the Discover your Genius: Workbook. This section will help you with Skills Identification and Goal Setting, a step-by-step process in helping you identify your personality profile, discovering all your hidden skills and abilities. It also takes you on a step-by-step process in creating and implementing goals.

I suggest that you read this book all the way through first, before turning to the workbook section to do the exercises. Once you have done the workbook, you will be able to use the information to write your cover letter and CV / Resume. You will also get a greater understanding about your personality which will give you more confidence when it comes to speaking. You will also get a clearer picture of what you want to do, and how to go about it in a step-by-step process.

As I have been working in the Education Business, as well as working in a Corporate environment as a General Manager in the Hospitality industry for over a decade, I have noticed that there is a great need to help youngsters, students and graduate students find their way as they leave their studies and enter into the big wide world, and into the work environment.

This book has come about to help students understand what they are up against, and to help them get ahead in life. There are so many school leavers and graduated students entering the work place each year who are going to compete against each other for the limited amount of job opportunities that are available, then also thrown into the mix, are job seekers who have already been in the work place, and have gained some work experience and are now looking to change their jobs for some reason. It is very competitive out there in the working arena.

This is a huge subject, however, what is in this book is a tiny bite to get you started, to set you on a path to discover more about who you are and how you can help yourself to achieve your goals. Please note that this book has been written with information from a Westerners point of view, and that things may be slightly different in each country or culture. This book is a quick guide to give job seekers an understanding of the process that you will have to go through. The interviewing process can be quite daunting and challenging when one is not prepared! So this book will help you do just that, "Prepare!"

"Life IS
One Big Learning Curve!
Let Life Happen,
But Be Aware
And Awake.

Learn
From These Lessons
And Experiences,
To Help
You Take Yourself
To A Higher Level!"
- Allan Rufus

Step one "Believe in yourself!"

1.

HOME PREPERATIONS

"Design your ideal life, and work towards it!" - Allan Rufus

- Deciding what you want to do

- Knowing your skills, talents, qualities and traits

- Job searching

- Application process

- Things to think about when creating your CV /Resume

- Creating your CV / Resume

- Know your CV / Resume backwards

- Writing a cover letter

- Getting directions

- Researching the company

- What to take with you

- Getting groomed

- What to wear

- Prepare mentally

- Social media sites

Deciding what you want to do

"Identify your passion in life, and do it!" - Allan Rufus

Deciding what type of job you would like to get and apply for is the first very important step in the breaking down process of possibilities to see what you would be good at / would be good for you! Some people know exactly what they want to do so the choice is easier, while others don't really know what to do, and things can become a lot tougher in deciding!

If you don't know what you want to do, or what job would be best suited for you, ask yourself some questions to narrow down the choices.

Do you want to work in-doors or out-doors? Do you want to work with animals or plants, or machines, or maybe both? Do you want to work on some type of transport system, or in a static location?

Do you want to work in a corporate environment, or in a more relaxed environment – In other words do you want to be a name or just a number? Do you want to work in an environment where you get to know every-ones name, or in an environment where it is impossible to know everyone?

Do you want to wear a suit and tie for men and suits

for ladies? Or do you want to wear more casual style clothing?

Do you like working more with your hands; landscaping, mechanic, building etc, or more with technology; computers, tablets, cameras, etc? Do you like to get dirty and messy or do you like to stay clean and tidy?

Do you want to work in the city or in a small village, countryside or isolated location?

Do you like working with people, or on your own?

How can you incorporate your studies with your hobbies and interests?

Choose your work environment very carefully, as this will become the place you spend more time at than anywhere else in your days, weeks, months and years ahead.

What I want you to do now is draw a circle on a piece of paper, and divide it up into 3 parts, 1st part - write down the number of hours you normally sleep, then the 2nd segment for the amount of free time you normally have, and the 3rd segment is for the time you work and travel. Now by doing this you will begin to see which segment you spend most of your life in, so it's extremely important to find a work environment that you will be happy in, as this is where you spend most of your 24 hours per day.

Now calculate those hours per week, per month and per year to see the amount of time you will be spending at the work place!

So for example, dividing up your 24 hour day into 3 pie pieces;

- 1st piece is your time at work and travelling = 10 hours

- 2nd piece is your free time/hobbies, house hold chores = 6 hours

- 3rd piece is your sleep time = 8 hours.

Which of these pie pieces are you spending most of your waking day in? Answer = Work and travel piece right?

So, it is vitally important to find the right working environment to work in, as this will affect your mind, health and well being, which will in turn effect your outer circumstances, your family, and maybe your social circles as well. Are you working to live or living to work?

Your 24 hour day!

Sleep

8 hrs

Work
and
Travel

10 hrs

Free time
House chores
6 hrs

So break your choices down into smaller pieces, and really think hard about what you want to do, and which direction you want to go in, as it will make your life a lot easier, and more pleasant in the long run!

REMEMBER, IF YOU DON'T KNOW WHAT YOU WANT, NO ONE CAN HELP YOU GET IT!!!

Common mistakes that can prevent you from getting the job search process done properly

- Not dedicating enough time to job searching. This should become your full time job until you get a job – So spend up to 8 hours a day if necessary. Diversify your search if need be

- Taking too many breaks and not searching, researching, tailor making your CV/ Resume with key words, doing follow ups of sent out CV /Resumes

- Rushing into the job search. Get advice from other people who have been in this same situation

- Letting frustration and negative emotions creep into your job searching. Stay positive and know that the perfect job will open up for you at the right time. Have patience if your applications are rejected and keep on being persistent and consistent

- Getting distracted from outside influences and social media

- Not taking enough time out to relax, and having a break for personal and social activities

Knowing your skills, talents, qualities and traits

"What good is knowledge if I don't put it into practice!"
- Allan Rufus

Remember that the job is really about you and what value you can bring to the company over and above the other people that will be interviewed. It's all about the skills you can offer them. They are looking for skills and the value you can bring to the business, and in return they will compensate you with a salary, incentives, perks and in some cases profit share of the yearly profits.

So you are actually selling YOU! (You are your brand – what are you known for?) So it's best to know you, your brand, your skills, your talents, your qualities and your traits.

Look at yourself as a sales person, and you are selling YOU!

Turn to page 84 for Discovering your Genius: Skills Identification and Goal Setting Workbook. The more effort you put into completing this workbook, the more you will come to know yourself, and the more confident you will become in yourself and your abilities.

ALLAN RUFUS

Why is it important to list your hard and soft skills in your CV / Resume?

When you go for an interview you are competing with others who may also have the same technical hard skills as you, so it is the set of soft skills, people skills, personal skills and social skills that you have that will be the deciding factor when the interviewer needs to make a choice between all the candidates.

Therefore, as a newly graduated student, where you may not have practical work experience, only theory, you need to back this up with your personality traits and your interpersonal and social people skills, after all it's how you interact with people that will give you the edge! In other words your character traits.

Also, recognize certain jobs may not need many soft skills, but the more you have the better your chances of getting that job!

Hard Skills

So what are hard skills? Hard skill are your theoretical learnt abilities, your education which has being learnt at school and University, as well as your experiences you have gained/achieved, which is brain powered. These skills can be measured.

Some examples:

- A Degree or Certificates

- Accounting

- Chemistry

- Finance

- Languages

- Mathematics

- Programming

- Machine operation

- Statistics

- Some type of development

- Some type of management

- Using computer software: word, excel, power point, photoshop etc

- Typing / Short hand / Taking minutes at meetings

- Etc

Soft Skills / People Skills / Interpersonal Skills

School leavers and graduated university students may or may not have the practical experience of using their hard skills in the work place yet, therefore they need to compensate that by having a large range (a stock of skills or types of behaviour that a person habitually uses) of soft skills / people skills which they can bring to the interviewers attention. This is where being "street wise" can help you a lot!

So, what are soft skills? Soft skills are not really learnt at school, but in your everyday environment. If you pay attention to what is going on around you, everything can become a great teacher to you, and you can pick up some great soft skills, good habits and great personal touches by watching other people in action. Become a people watcher to see what they are doing and saying, and if they are good qualities, add them to your character, if you see or feel any that are not good, look inside yourself to see if you have those negative qualities, and work on getting rid of them!

These skills cannot really be measured, they are subjective skills. These are the skills in which you relate to others, or people skills. Some examples on page 135 in the Skills Identification Workbook.

Now you need to ask yourself a few questions in the strategy you want to use in your resume, "Do I want to be a specialist? Or do I want to be a generalist?"

If you know exactly what you are looking for, and have done your research on the company you are applying to, then you can match your skill set to what the company's requirements are, you don't need to add all your skills, only add the skills you think might be useful and compatible for each job description. However, if you are not sure, and you are applying for a job where the company has hundreds of employees, then your broad base of skills would be beneficial to the company.

You can also state your primary skills which you are proficient in first, then state your secondary skills which you are competent in. You don't want to congest your resume with unrelated skills, so do your research first before sending your resume.

Job searching

Job searching is the act of looking for a job. So where does a person begin job searching? There are numerous outlets where you can start looking for your perfect job!

Start to get a list together of all the possible companies you would like to apply to. You may have to do this on a weekly basis until you find that perfect job you are looking for. Start by sending your Cover Letter and CV / Resume to the top companies on your list. Don't send your documents to all the potential companies. Tailor make each Cover Letter and Resume to what the company is looking for, or as close to it as possible. Keep notes on what you think is working and not working, so next time you can make adjustments to your documents. Strategize carefully per each application and try get as much feedback as possible.

You can send your CV / Resume into job agencies, or post them online. Please be aware of the places you leave your CV/Resume, don't just place your information anywhere and everywhere. Have discernment, and watch out for scams!

Online www places to look for employment and place your resume:

- Job search engines sites/ student job search engines

- Internet job/career online agencies

- LinkedIn jobs

- Craig's list jobs

- Social sites

- Email someone you admire, tell them why you admire them, send them your resume, and ask them for any advice they can offer you to help you get ahead

Physical places:

- Networking with friends, family and acquaintances

- Job agencies

- Newspapers, local, national and international

- Magazines

- Go to companies you feel you would like to work at

- Notice boards

Application process

Writing a great and outstanding professional cover letter and CV/ Resume is vital in your application process preparations. TIP: Put yourself in the interviewer's shoes. They are not mind readers, and they will go by what they are seeing and reading! They know what they are looking for, and does your application match it or come close to it?

The role of these 2 tools are to convince the company / interviewer to invite you in for an interview. These 2 tools are just the beginning to get your foot in the door, then the real skill is when you are face to face with the interviewer/s in selling your skills, abilities, brand, knowledge, talents, attitude and qualities.

Take your time in tailor making your Cover Letter and CV / Resume as they will end up in one of three places. The interviewer is going to have a quick read of your letter, and they are going to put it into;

- The rubbish bin,

- The maybe pile or

- The definitely pile.

You want to <u>tailor make</u> your cover letter and CV/Resume to suit the job you are applying for, so get it put in the <u>definitely pile!</u>

Remember, you are trying to **<u>stand out</u>** from the crowd. Be creative as possible. In certain industries you can create graphic and video CV's to add to your uniqueness!

Bring awareness of all your achievements, and don't be vague about them. The employer will want to know what value you can bring to them from what you have learnt in your studies at university / or from your previous employer/ or any projects you have completed.

If you have had a job before, tell them how you added value to your last employer, for example, how you saved them money, how you introduced a new time saving and money saving system, a great way to interact with clients etc. Attaching your achievements gives the interviewer great insight on the value that you can bring to the company. **Boast about / attract attention to your achievements and abilities!**

It is the age of the internet and email, and it is so easy to be like everyone else and upload it on internet sites and/or send it by email. This is fine, but you may not really get noticed that much. BUT, if you post it or even better, hand deliver your documents to the company, you may even get to meet the HR Personal interviewer 1st hand, where you will be remembered more clearly, as you can make that first impression before the interview! Your documents will be physically in their hands, and not a copy on their computer!

So, tailor make, and adapt your cover letter and CV/ Resume for each different vacancy on offer. Make it relevant to the job offer. Don't be general and generic, in other words, don't send out the same Cover Letter and CV /Resume to every job offer!

How do you do this? Simply by adding in key skills which would be useful for certain jobs, and adding achievements relating to this type of work. Do your research on each company you are going to apply to!

Things to think about when creating your CV /Resume

Appearance – Your CV / Resume is mainly about the content you place in it. You want it to be easily read and visually appealing.

Use a font and size that is readable, and friendly to the eye. Use a combination of short paragraphs and bullets to display your work experiences, accomplishments and achievements.

Text:

- Make sure there are NO spelling mistakes, and the grammar is correct

- Use action words (Verbs). Things you have done, contributed, developed, reorganized, resolved etc

- Good fonts to use are **Arial** or **Verdana** size 12

Remember,

The 1st impression is

EVERYTHING!!!

Creating your CV / Resume

Q: What is a CV / Resume?

A: A CV (Curriculum Vitae) and a Resume are documents on which you write down your education, experiences, achievements and skills.

This is what you send to a potential employer to get their attention so they call you in for an interview. Then it is up to you to sell your skills to them, and persuade them that you are the person they are looking for to help their company function well and prosper.

Q: What is the difference between a CV and a Resume?

 A CV is used mostly when applying for academic work, scientific and research positions and when applying for fellowships and grants. (Fellowships cover educational and living expenses, and grants cover specific project expenses.) What should be included in your CV is your educational /academic background as well as any teaching

/ research experience. All your publications, presentations, awards, honors, and any other relevant information.

A Resume is normally 1 or 2 pages and is short and to the point.

- Contact details

- Objective

- Education and Qualifications

- Achievements and Awards

- Work History and Experiences

- Professional and Personal Skills and any other relevant skills

- Hobbies and Interests

- Contactable details (Name and either phone number or email address) from last job.

Make sure you have a professional email address, for example johnsmith@*****.com and not a fun playful one like partyanimal@*****.com. If you don't have a professional email address, open one for your professional emails. It is best to have an email address with your name, or part name in it. You can find a resume template on page 75.

Key words should be used when writing a cover letter and CV / Resume.

Scanning technology is utilized on the internet today, and up-loaded internet CV/Resumes are scanned looking at keywords and key phrases as well as particular skills, qualifications and expertise needed for the job requirement in which the employer is looking for.

Companies and recruiters are searching for key attributes, and they scan your documents looking for them. So even though you might be the right candidate for the job, if your cover letter and CV/Resume is lacking key words, you won't even be noticed, so you need to add these key words to **attract maximum attention**. Only add keywords to match your skills and abilities.

How to get the interviewers attention with a good CV / Resume

- Focus on what you want, don't be general

- Make sure your opening summary is informative, without over doing it. Include your qualifications, and some back ground about you. Be precise about your experience and collective knowledge in relation to the job

- List your most recent jobs at the top of the

page, if you have any

- Don't list everything you have done, summarize it in a carefully worded style

- For newly graduated students, add your information about your degree, internship, academic honours, etc

- Be specific about your skill set

- Imagine you are the interviewer, and ask yourself what would I want to see and read in connection with this job

Things that should NOT be added to your CV / Resume

- Salary

- Physical attributes: weight, height, skin colour, health, pregnancy status (Unless specifically needed for the role in tv, stage, modeling, etc)

- Origin – Ethnicity: Culture, nationality, race (however, if you are working in a foreign country you will be asked some of these)

- Marital status: Whether you are married, intend to be married, if you have children, what sexual orientation you are – straight, gay, lesbian, bisexual, transgendered

- Religion

- Political affiliation: Which party you support

Mistakes to be aware of when writing your CV / Resume

- Spelling mistakes

- Bad grammar

- Incorrect contact details

- Leaving out important information

- Having a scattered CV. Make sure it is logically in order and in a step-by-step time frame

- Fonts – best to keep to one or two, if using two, keep it uniform so not unpleasant on the eyes

- Having one CV / Resume for all job applications – Tailor make it for each different job application

- Not highlighting your accomplishments

Know your CV / Resume backwards

Learn your CV/ Resume until you know it backwards. University students, know your subjects, grades etc. If you have worked before, know every date, company, dates you worked for each company, what you did there, who you worked for, the person at your previous company that can be contacted as a reference. Your skills and qualifications, your strengths and weaknesses.

Writing a cover letter

Q: What is the function of a cover letter?

A: The function of a cover letter is to get you an interview!

Realize that, because there are so many people applying for the same job as you, the cover letter is one way to filter out all the people that the company does not want to waste their time and money on! This is why a cover letter is so important, as this is the first point of contact with the company you are applying to and with the interviewer conducting the recruitment process. This letter if done correctly will get you an interview. **Strategize this letter carefully and use your answers from the workbook once you have completed it!** You can find a template on page 73.

Getting directions once you have been selected

Make sure you get the correct details, contact person's name, number and address where the interview is going to take place. Write them down on your notepad that you are taking with you to the interview.

Have a good look on a map where you are going to go, and even print it, or write down the directions so you cannot get lost, and you won't be late for the interview! If you are late for the interview, it won't set a good example for your time management skills, and may even cost you the job. BE PREPARED and BE EARLY!!!

Researching the company you are going to see

With today's modern technology it should be easy to find out information about a company you wish to apply to. Also remember it is just as easy for a company to search for you on the internet!

Before submitting your cover letter and CV / Resume, do some research on the company. What is their philosophy, business strategy, their ethics and what do they actually do!

What type of environment they work in, where is their office/ offices, do they operate locally or internationally, how many people do they employ. What size is the company and are you going to be a name or a number there.

After doing your research, you may find you don't want to work in that environment. Or you might find it is perfect for you, and then you are more prepared for the interview as you understand a bit more about the dynamics of the company.

What type of clothing will you have to wear to both the interview and to work if offered the position.

What to take with you: **<u>BE PREPARED</u>**

Preparing yourself for a job interview is vital! Make sure you have all your documents and information you may need to give to the interviewer, or may have to leave with the company you are going to see. In some cases you may need more than 1 copy, especially if you are going to work through an employment agency, they may require a copy, and the company may require a copy of these same documents. However, saying that, it is now very easy to send these things via email, or carry them on a USB stick. But be prepared, in case the interviewer does not have your documents in-front of them. This will show you are prepared for any situation. Make sure they are kept neatly and in order in some type of folder to prevent them getting damaged.

Things to take with you: Remember, 1st impression is everything! You may not be asked for any of these things but always be prepared!

- A Positive Attitude and Mind Set

- Your CV / Resume

- Relevant Certificates, sometimes originals will want to be seen, and NOT copies. <u>NEVER</u> leave your originals, only copies of them

- Transcripts from your University

- References. Professional References with contact details.

- ID or Passport

- A police clearance certificate if in a foreign country (If you are planning to work outside your country, get a police clearance certificate from your home country before you leave, and take it with you!)

- A few ID or Passport size pictures of yourself neatly dressed

- Bank Details

- Your Contact Details

- Driver's License if going for a driving position

- Directions and Instructions you have been given from company

- Pen and notepad – Write down the person's name you need to meet

- Work Samples. Physical samples, or a presentation on a electronic device.

- Your Portfolio that is organized in an orderly way

- A list of questions to ask so you don't forget anything you want to find out

What NOT to take:

- Other people

- Food or drink

- If you take your phone, either turn it off or put it on silent

- A scruffy bag

Getting groomed

The 1st impression is most important, and can be the decider for you getting the job or not! These tips below may or may not be suitable for the job you are going to! Use your discretion.

- Make sure your hair is clean and tidy

- Get your hair cut or present it in a professional and accepted manner

- Make sure you are shaved /neatly groomed

- Make sure your nails are clean, and well groomed and if painted, they are well painted with no patches or chipped pieces

- Wear deodorant, but don't overdo the smell with perfumes and scents, this can be very off putting to the interviewer.

- If you are going to wear makeup, don't overdo it and maybe wear neutral colours

- Brush your teeth, and don't have smelly breath

- Clean your ears

What to wear

Again use your discretion here! Be yourself, be polite and wear what you are comfortable in and allow your true character to come out! Your dress code is communicating about who you are!

Depending on what type of job you are applying for, and the image of the company, determines the types of clothing you need to wear for your interview. Always be neat and tidy! We know that "image" does play a large part in society, and this perception is a powerful factor always at play. However, if you decide not to go the suit look or you choose to wear something outrageous, just be comfortable in your shoes, and let this shine out of who you are, as after all it's the complete package the company is looking for. Have you got the skills and can you do what they are looking for and more? Then clothing may not play a deciding factor.

If you are applying for an office job, then you may be required to wear a suit and tie, or a long sleeve shirt with a tie and for ladies, a long skirt, or long pants with a suitable top that is not low around the neck. It has been said that red is not a good colour to wear to an interview ladies!

Make sure your shoes are clean, and polished if need be!

Things to be aware of:

- Don't overdo your makeup ladies

- Cover all tattoos if possible

- Not too much jewelry

- No hats, unless appropriate

Prepare Mentally

"The power of the mind is an incredible tool

to be used wisely!" - Allan Rufus

Work smart, not hard. So, do your mind work first.

Once you have finished writing your cover letter and CV/ Resume, read it until you know it backwards. Then sit quietly in a place you will not be disturbed and visualize the whole process that you will be going through in relation to your job interview. Start from you preparing your clothes, placing all you need to take with you into your bag, having a shower and grooming yourself, getting dressed, leaving your accommodation, taking your transport to the venue, see yourself as confident, happy and positive. See yourself arriving at the venue and introducing yourself to the receptionist, or person you will meet, see yourself greeting the interviewer with a big smile on your face showing excitement and enthusiasm at being there, seeing your good body language, sitting down, taking out your paper / pen and notepad, placing them on the table in front of you, speaking to the interviewer, smiling, being confident, showing interest, good eye contact, answering any questions that are asked in a confident and clear manner, telling the interviewer about yourself, your qualifications, your skills and asking the interviewer your questions. Ask when the applicant can expect to be contacted about the position. See yourself thanking them for a great interview, asking them for their contact details, putting all your papers into your bag, standing up straight, shaking hands in a good firm grip, walking out with a straight body and head and chin straight forward. See yourself saying good bye to the receptionist or other people who may be around, see yourself smiling and being confident and walking outside. Take a deep breath and let go!

The psychology to this is that you are placing yourself in that situation before you get there. You may or may not know the whole set up, it matters not. Just see yourself setting the intention. If you are having problems with visualization, think of something in the past, and what you see is your "body" there, doing what you were doing, now you can use that same technique to send your "body" into the future to create the outcome you want, then when you go to the interview, you already know what is going to happen, and this makes you more relaxed with the process.

THIS IS A VERY POWERFUL TECHNIQUE THAT CAN BE USED DAILY IN CREATING THE THINGS YOU WANT IN YOUR LIFE. SEE IT, FEEL IT, KNOW IT AND BE IT!

Social media sites

With today's social media sites on the internet, the interviewer may type your name into a search engine to see what comes up. So tell the truth as any inconsistencies will show up. They will be able to see your blogs, facebook, twitter, youtube and other social media accounts that you have. So make sure there isn't anything on them that will prove you to be unsuitable for getting the job!

Creating a blog of some kind is a way to brand yourself, and market yourself, and it can be shown to the interviewer so they get a clear sense of who you are and what you are capable of doing and creating.

You can see there is a lot to think about and to do in your preparations at home. These preparations are vital to get correct, and to memories, which will then lead you and help you in the next part of the process, **the action**!

"To get anywhere I have to get up and go towards where I want to go!" - **Allan Rufus**

Step two "Trust in yourself!"

2.
AT THE INTERVIEW

"I am the actor, script writer, clothes designer of my life and the world is my stage!" - Allan Rufus

- What to expect

- What to remember while in the interview

- Business Etiquette

- First Impressions

- Body Language

- Greetings

- How to have a good interview

- Understand the interviewers agenda

- Branding yourself / Selling your skills

- What questions are most asked

- What questions to ask

- What questions not to ask

- How to negotiate your salary

- What questions to ask after the offer

- When you should NOT take the job

- Responsibilities

"Trust in yourself and be ready for everything!"

What to expect

In many countries employment laws forbid discrimination as part of the interview based on your race, religion, age, gender, and marital status and constitutes illegal hiring practices. However, this does not apply in all countries, so be prepared to answer these types of questions if they arise!

You are going to go through a process where the interviewer may start explaining the job position, then ask you questions to find out who you are and what you can do. You will also be given an opportunity to ask some questions back. The salary will either be negotiated or a set salary structure will be offered. You may or may not be offered the job immediately, as the interviewer may want to go through all the applicants first and then decide who is the best candidate. If offered the job, you can either say yes, or ask for 24hours to think about if the job suits your needs!

Business Etiquette and What to remember while in the interview

- Dress appropriately

- Don't be late, be punctual

- Be professional

- Be confident

- Always be polite

- Greet people with a smile and look them in the eyes

- Use a firm hand shake when greeting people

- Only sit when invited to

- Place your bag on the floor next to you, don't keep it on your lap, as you want to look comfortable, take out your note book and other documents at this stage and keep them on your lap or put them on the table in front of you

- Make sure your phones and tablet etc are on silent or off

- Speak clearly

- Always pay attention to your body language. Body language plays a big role in the language you are talking, it speaks through its actions. So make sure you are always sitting and standing upright

- Smile, be positive, and enjoy the process

First Impressions

First impression are everything and they last, so therefore it is vital that when you meet the interviewer, and in fact anybody in general, you want to do so in a manner that will leave a good uplifting impression of yourself!

Your 5 senses as well as the interviewer's 5 senses will be identifying each other;

- 1. What one looks like – **Visual**

- 2. What one sounds like – **Auditory**

- 3. The touch (hand shake)- **Kinesthetic**

- 4. What one smells like – **Olfactory**

- 5. The **gut feeling** which comes from the solar plexus. The gut feeling is never wrong, so learn to listen to it and trust it! The gut feeling picks up the energy vibration the other person is giving off, and interprets this energy into a feel good, or a not feel good energy response.

So, what can we do to leave a good first impression?

Firstly, for visual effect, have good body posture, have a genuine smile on your face, and let your eyes smile, as your eyes are the window to your soul, and people are always looking into each other's eyes. A person can tell a lot about another person just by looking into the eyes. Be well groomed, neat and tidy. Wear the appropriate clothing and footwear for the occasion. Are your clothes colourful and bright and fresh looking, or dark, dull and uninspiring? Jewelry and tattoos can also leave an impression, so ask yourself – "Is this the occasion to wear a lot of jewelry and show off my tattoos?"

Secondly, for auditory effect, be very aware of what you are saying, what words you are using, are they positive and uplifting or not? Are you leaving the person you are talking to feeling up-lifted and excited about what you are saying or not?

Thirdly, Kinesthetic is our touch. When you greet, and shake hands, do so with your hand facing straight and not upwards to show submissiveness, or downwards to show dominance. Make sure your hand shake has a firm grip and not a bone crunching or sloppy fish hand shake grip. Best to shake with the same pressure as the interviewer.

Fourthly, Olfactory is our smell. Make sure you smell clean and fresh, and don't overdo the deodorant, or perfume. You may think it smells great, but if it is over bearing, it will make the interviewer uncomfortable, and your interview may be cut really short, and you may not be given a chance to sell yourself and your skill set.

Fifthly, Gut feeling is everything! The energy imprint we leave on the persons solar plexus will determine a yes, maybe or no to employing you! The gut feeling is picking up all the non-verbal language that is flowing between you and the other person. So, leave a good impression or a good feeling by having a good happy, uplifting vibration flowing from your being, as most people react on that, especially intuitive people, and entrepreneurs. You may not have all the hard skills they are looking for, but your soft skills along with the good feeling they have of you may just land you that job offer!

Body Language

Body language is a vast subject on its own, and maybe you should read up more about it, which will not only help you in winning over someone, but also helping you become aware of what the subtle message is that the other person is portraying in connection to you!

Here are some basic things that you should be aware of when going to a job interview;

- As you walk into the company, make sure you are stand straight upright, standing tall! (Tuck your lower back inwards, and push your chest outwards in front of you)

- Keep your chin level or slightly upwards

- Keep yourself open by not folding, crossing your arms, legs and feet. This cuts off the energy flow

- Keep your hands facing inwards or upwards and not backwards or downwards

- When shaking hands, make sure your hand is facing straight and not upwards or downwards, as this will reflect if you are submissive or dominate and you don't want to appear to be either

- Have good eye contact with the interviewer when talking, but don't stare when not talking, as this will make them feel very uncomfortable

- When sitting, sit up straight, keep the spine straight, and chin up and keep your feet firmly on the ground next to each other (ground yourself)

- Face the interviewer at all times

- A good thing to try and do is mirror the interviewer, watch their body language, and follow them but in a very subtle way, don't make it look like you are mocking them

- A smile goes a long way, and it shows you are interested in what they are saying and comfortable in the situation / circumstances. A smile also brings a feeling of happiness which you want to portray. This will also stop you frowning and having other negative or serious facial features

- You can talk with your hands but don't wave them around wildly and don't fidget. When they are still, best keep them relaxed and on your lap

- Notice where your hands, fingers and feet are pointing, as it is a great indicator of where your energy is flowing, so best keep your feet facing the interviewer, and don't point at the interviewer with one finger, rather have an open palm pointing towards them, with all your fingers slightly apart

- When standing up, keep a straight back, while smiling, again shake the interviewers hand in a firm grip and say thank you for their time and the interview while looking them in the eyes, and walk out with an upright posture and your chin up, no matter how the interview went

Greetings

Manners are everything!!!

A "please", and a "thank-you" are two small but imperative sayings, which have huge implications. They would be very welcomed and noticeable if used or not used. They are the first and last indicator of your people skills, or lack of!

How to have a good interview

> *"Attune into your own strengths!"* - Allan Rufus

Be yourself, meaning just be the best you can be! You have done your preparation, you understand who you are, why you are there, and what you are trying to achieve, and now it is time to deliver your "sales pitch and sell your skills!

Take a few good deep breaths and relax and enjoy the process and the interaction and build rapport with the interviewer. Building rapport with the interviewer is crucial and must be a high priority in your approach. Without good rapport, there is not much chance of getting the position!

Listen with intent to what the interviewer is saying, and if you don't understand, ask them to repeat it again until you do understand. When it is your turn to speak, be clear and precise, have a structured way of presenting yourself, your skills and what you can offer the company, and offer examples of things you have achieved.

Understand the interviewers agenda

What does this mean? The interviewers agenda is to find a person who is most skilled and suitable for the position on offer so the company goals and targets can be reached and exceeded. They know what they need, and what they are looking for and now they are interviewing people to fill that criteria, or to get as close to it as possible.

The process;

- 1st step – Now that your tailored cover letter and CV / Resume has grabbed their attention, you have been placed in the "definitely interview these people" pile or the maybe pile

- 2nd step – They want to see you in the physical! They want to see your outer appearance, your inner character and what skills you have to offer

- Once all the applicants have been interviewed, they will decide which person closely fulfils the requirements they are looking for in hard skills, soft skills as well as character

They will more than likely start telling you about the position, and what is expected, then they are going to focus their attention on you. They are going to ask you lots of questions to find out more about you, your hard and soft skills and your competence. They will take notice of how you are answering the questions, including your tone of voice which says more than what you actually say, so make sure your tone is uplifting, positive and full of energy. They will listen for the words you choose to use, and how confident you are in what you are saying. They will also watch your shift in body language as you answer the questions as body language works in a subtle way and unless you are aware of it, it tells exactly if what you are saying equals to the way you really feel about what you are saying. They will be listening out for keywords that are needed and associated with that position, so answer in a way that will show you can bring value and benefit to that position.

They will have an idea of what they are looking for, and so it is important to be truthful and honest, and don't think anything may be too small to comment on or say. It may be that small comment that gets you the job. Remember you are there to let them know who you are, and what you can do, and how you are willing to learn and that you are a very quick learner of new systems!

The interviewer will want to find out about your work history, education history, your personality, your style of working and to see if you can work under pressure.

They need to know that you can not only do the job, but do it better than anyone else that they are going to interview. They need to know that you can bring great value to the company and to the position. Remember, it is their reputation on the line if things go well, or not well in hiring the applicant! They will be looking for someone who can multi-task, and multi-task well.

Many companies no longer look at the University Degree grades anymore, as that is only a piece of paper with hard skills on it. What they are looking for is the persons character and soft skills they have to do the job well.

Example: Theory VS Application. A sales person can have good or even outstanding qualifications on paper, but they do not have the people skills to close the deal when dealing with real people.

Paper skills does not equal real life experience skills.

The interviewer could also be trying to find out whether you are an extrovert, an introvert or an ambiversion person. In other words to see what your relationship to others, and yourself will be like. (to find out more information about this. http://en.wikipedia.org/wiki/Extraversion_and_intr oversion)

Branding yourself / Selling your skills

"The strength of my skills depends on the purity and clarity of my mind!" - Allan Rufus

Ultimately what you are doing in the interview is selling your brand, which are your skills, talents, qualities, and qualifications.

This is what makes us all unique, and this is what makes us an individual! There are no two people alike due to our upbringing, our different cultures, lifestyle, our habits and our teachers who take many forms from parents, to friends, to society, to school and university teachers and professors, as well as religious leaders.

So this is where you can now display all you have as a package to the interviewer, and if they like what you have, and they can get you at the right salary, then you will get hired. Then it is up to you to produce the results, and when you do this beyond their expectations, then you have a good chance of getting a good salary increase and maybe even get promoted. A company does not want to get rid of or lose a person who has a good overall package that they bring to the company.

The greater amount of proficient skills you have, the greater the chance of being hired and looked after to keep you at the company.

So take your time, and really think hard about what your brand is, what are your skills, your talents, your qualities, your traits and your qualifications. Write them all down, and don't think something is not important, as that thing could be what the employer is looking for to complement your other skills and that could give you the edge over the other interviewees.

Questions

These following questions are commonly asked in interviews, so be prepared to answer them!

"Be yourself; everyone else is already taken!" – Oscar Wilde

Here are some common questions that you may be asked, so think about the best way you would answer these questions:

- Q. Tell me about and how do you describe yourself!

- Q. What are your strengths?

- Q. What are your weaknesses?

- Q. What makes you qualified for this position?

- Q. Where do you see yourself in 5 - 10 years?

- Q. Why do you want to work with this company?

- Q. Why should I take the risk employing you?

- Q. How do you evaluate success?

- Q. What sort of salary are you looking for?

- Q. What is the number 1 ability a person should have to succeed in this role?

- Q. How do you handle pressure and stress?

- Q. What motivates you?

- Q. What are you passionate about?

- Q. What is your dream job?

- Q. Why should I NOT hire you?

Do some research on the internet to see what other questions you might be asked, and get some ideas and advice on how to answers them back.

Research is KEY! Go to an internet search engine and type in:

- Job interview questions and answers for new graduate students
- How to answer the Greatest Weakness Job interview question
- How to Answer Job Interview Question for Graduate students
- How to Answer Job Interview Question for Graduate students PDF
- Common interview questions for fresh graduates

If you have had a previous job, then you will be asked about it, and why you left it. So prepare yourself to answer questions on it, and about your previous boss, manager, the work environment etc.

Once you have completed the Discovering Your Genius Workbook on page 84 you will have greater insight and awareness of yourself and your abilities, and this will make answering these questions easier.

What questions to ask

"If you don't ask, you don't get! - Allan Rufus

The 1st line of business I ever learnt was "If you don't ask, you don't get". So, I learnt to ask questions and ask for things. The reality is, the worst thing that can happen is the other person says "No!"

Why should you ask questions? Well, you are looking to work at a company that suits you. You spend more time at the office than anywhere else, so it is important to find a position that you will be happy in, and you will enjoy spending your time there. A happy worker makes for good production!

By asking questions then it will also show the interviewer that you are serious about looking for a position that suits you, and not just there to get a job!

Interviewees who ask questions are more likely to get the job, than those who don't ask questions. By not asking questions can show you are not really interested in the job.

Some questions you may want to ask:

- Could you tell me more about the position on offer including the responsibilities and what a normal day is like. Is this a new position or was there someone previously employed?

How many positions are open? Where is the location for this position?

- How long was/were the previous employees in this job? (find out if there is a high staff turnover, if there is, then this is an indicator of maybe things are not so good here!)

- What hours are expected per day/week and is there overtime available for hours worked over basic time?

- Can you tell me about the official holidays and leave structure? Are there any periods that one cannot take personal leave? Does the company operate during public holidays and will I be expected to work?

- How many people work in this department, and what is the reporting structure?

- Is there a dress code, and if so, are the clothes supplied?

- Can you tell me some things about the CEO/General Manager/ My manager, and what to expect from them?

- Is there an opportunity for growth and advancement in the company/companies

- Are there other branches locally or

internationally, and is relocation possible? Who sorts out the relevant visas?

- What is the termination policy? How many months/weeks must either party give the other party? What happens if either side breaches the agreement?

- What are the good things about working for this company?

- When will you let the right applicant know about the position, and when is the start date?

- Will you inform all unsuccessful applicants and on which date?

- Is there anything else you would like to know from me?

You may have other questions you would like to ask, and realize that not all the suggested questions in this book would be appropriate to ask. These are guide lines for you!

Other more serious questions to ask, which can help you either stand out in the interview, or will give you feedback so you are more prepared for the future! In other words you are looking for feedback about how well you have done in your interview!

- Are there any gaps in my qualifications that I need to be aware of?

- Are there any reasons that I am not fully qualified for this position?

- Have I said or done anything that prevents me getting hired?

- Have I said or done anything in the interview that is inconsistent with what you are looking for in the person you want to hire?

What questions not to ask

- What does this company do?

- Did I get the job? (ONLY if the interview goes really well and you feel you have had good rapport with the interviewer, then maybe ask in a joking manner!)

How to negotiate your salary

The bottom line is that you want to be paid your worth.

The company will be trying to keep their salary costs down while trying to get the best skills required to do the job effectively.

This part of the interview may be uncomfortable for some people. This is why it is important to be prepared, and have all the information at your disposal, to show you are efficient, can add value to the company, have an understanding of what is needed to get the job done well.

Although as a newly graduated student, more times than not the salary will be set at a particular rate, however in some cases you may have a rare skill/talent/quality that is needed and in demand, where you can negotiate your salary. You don't want to out price yourself, but you don't want to sell yourself short either. You also need find out the going rates in your location for your chosen field.

Ask yourself before you go to the interview:

- "How many qualifications and/or skills do I have for this role and what work experience do I have?"

- "What am I worth?"

- "What are my living expenses?"

You may want to let the interviewer bring up this subject, unless the interview is finished and they have not spoken to you about the salary involved. If the interviewer does bring up the subject of salary very early in the interview, and asks what you want, it may be best to say you need some more information about the role you would have to perform, and what is the value of the role, and the budget for the position.

Have an idea of the amount you would like to get, and when the interview asks you how much you want, you can ask them to give you the salary range they are offering for the position.

Then you can give them the amount you think you are worth and at the same time nodding your head in a subtle way to say "yes" you are worth it!. Also have an explanation why you think you are worth that amount, and what value you will bring to the company. Highlighting your qualifications, experience, skills, accomplishments etc.

If the amount you would like does not equal the amount offered, but you feel it is a company your can grow with, and learn a lot from and it's a place to get that valuable experience from, you can then ask about other benefits, for example:

- Are there bonuses attached to this position?

- Is there any profit share?

- Negotiate on extra days off / holidays

- Can you work from home, if applicable

- Reduced hours

- Does the company offer any other perks –
  Medical aid, work clothing, housing benefits,
  travel expenses, phone allowance, meals
  provided

AS I SAY "IF YOU DON'T ASK "YOU DON'T GET!"

If the interviewer say "We don't negotiate!" then
leave it at that and don't ask again!

Always remain amicable and open to negotiation and
compromise. Don't become aggressive, abrupt or
defensive. You need to show you have flexibility and
the company may show flexibility too to come to
some arrangement that is good for both you and the
employer.

What questions you may want to ask after the offer

- When do you require an answer for the job
  offer?– You may want to go home and think
  about it, and maybe discuss it with friends and
  family

- Can I have the job description, salary, benefits
  and any other relevant documents in writing
  before I start?

- When would you want me to start?

- Who should I report to?

- If I have any other questions, who can I speak to?

- Is there a parking space available for me to park my car or bike? (If you have a vehicle and will be driving to work)

When you should NOT take the job

Sometimes you will get a feeling that all is not well, and you should listen to that gut feeling, as it is never wrong. What else to watch out for that will be an indicator that all is not well with that job:

- If your interviewer is very late

- They have not read your CV / Resume

- Vague title

- Vague information

- No clear job description

- The interviewer is asking lots of personal questions

- The interviewer cannot answer your questions properly

- Different interviewers giving you different information, if you have been called in again for another interview

- No physical location for the company

- No information about the company

- If you have a bad feeling about the interview, after the interview do a search and look for any comments reviews about the company or persons involved with the company

- The interviewer is saying bad things about the previous person who was doing the job

- If the body language of the interviewer is negative

- The interviewer does not give you the time and respect you deserve in the interview

- If you are offered the job, and you are told to say to people phoning or coming into the location, "the owner/boss/manager is not available!"

- The job position forces you to go against your integrity, work ethic or objectives

- If there is a high turnover of staff

- If you are offered the job straight away, are they desperate to fill the job? Why?

- If you need to pay money before you get the job

Responsibilities

Once you have been offered the job it then becomes your responsibility to live up to your successful interview expectations. You do this by working with total integrity, honesty and commitment.

The interviewer has taken the chance on employing you, now it is time to show them and the company that they have made the correct decision. It is your reputation as well as the interviewers reputation in the limelight.

Take the time to learn as much as you possibly can in that company, and I don't just mean learn what you can in connection to your position, I mean learn as much as you can from all departments, as this will make you more employable when you decide to move onto another company, or even if you want to open your own business.

<u>Remember, it is how you apply your knowledge and skills set that makes you successful and indispensible!</u>

If need be, volunteer yourself when the company is looking for people to help them out even if it is in a different field to which you are involved in. You may have to say to them that you have no knowledge in that field, but you are willing to learn and help out! Not only will this improve your skills, it will also show the "boss" you are hands on and you are motivated and have a desire to learn new things. This approach may just keep you employed when downsizing in a company happens.

My Motto – "As long as I learn something new every day, it doesn't matter how large or small that something is, because it is something I never knew before to add to my knowledge, and character!"
– Allan Rufus

Step three "Acknowledge yourself!"

3.
AFTER THE INTERVIEW

There are a few things you can do after the interview which may help you get the job or help you prepare for other job interviews:

- Quickly write down your thoughts, feelings, what you thought went well, and what you thought did not go well

- Write a thank-you note

- Follow up

Quickly write down your thoughts, feeling and what you thought went well, and what you thought did not go well!

Ok, now that the interview is finished, sit down for a moment and take out your notebook and pen and jot down your feelings, what you thought went well, and what you thought did not go well. This will be important feedback for you for future reference when applying for another job interview, and can also help you bring awareness to what you have to improve on for next time, not only in a business environment, but maybe also in a social setting.

- How did you feel when you came out of the interview?

- Did you present yourself well?

- Did you answer all the questions well? If not, which questions?

- Did your body language stay consistent during the interview?

- Did you say anything or do anything that you should not have said or done?

- Did you forget to bring something important to the interview?

- Were you fully prepared enough for the interview?

- Were there any questions asked, and you couldn't give a great answer to?

- Were there any questions you asked, but didn't really get the answers you were looking for, and is there another way of asking them?

- Were your clothes appropriate for the setting of the interview?

- Were you relaxed, or nervous and full of anxiety?

- What do you feel you could have done better?

- How long was the interview?

- Did you have good eye contact and rapport with the interviewer? If not, what can you do better next time?

- Are you going to come back for a 2nd interview, and if so, what should you prepare for?

- Is there anything you have noticed about the other interviewees that you can learn from or take with you to help you next time you go for an interview?

- Was this the right type of job, setting, environment that you really would like to work in?

- What did you learn, that you can use in another job interview?

- What comes to mind that you can write in your follow up letter to the interviewer that maybe you did not talk about, or did not come out clearly when you did speak about it?

Write a thank you note

By writing a thank you note, you will not only keep your name alive in the interviewers mind, you will also make an impression and show you are good at following up your commitments.

What should you include in this letter? Keep it short and to the point! You can find a template on page 79

- Thank them for their time and the interview.

- You can also add in anything you forgot to mention in the interview

- Reiterate you interest in the job

- Show you are enthusiastic about working at the company

Follow up

If you don't hear back from the company after about 7 days, write a follow up letter to the interviewer asking about the position, to see if it is still available, or has it be filled. Be courteous and polite.

You can also state you are still interested in the position if available, or if that position has been filled, do they have any other position available that you could be considered for? As you would really like to work at that company.

5.
A CHECK LIST TO TAKE WITH YOU

*"Do the best you can
with what you've got right in front of you!" - Allan Rufus*

By having a check list with you it can help you feel more relaxed, as you will not forget to do anything that is important to do!

Job Interview Check List!

Home preparations
- Look for those jobs that most interests you
- Read the job requirements carefully and on a separate piece of paper write them down on one side, so you know exactly what the company is looking for. Then on the opposite side write down your hard and soft skills, qualities, talents and traits. Know what they want, and know what you have got, so you can tailor make your CV/ Resume to get as close as possible to what they are looking for from the interviewees
- Research those companies as best as possible to find out who and what they are, and find out who they compete with – their competition
- Research what you are worth salary wise, so you have an idea where to negotiate from. Education, Skills, talents etc VS Experience and your living expenses
- Prepare personal statements and answers for you, as you will more than likely be asked the questions "Tell me about yourself?", "Where do you see

yourself in 5 - 10 years?), "Why should we employ/take a risk on you?", "What can you bring to the company that will be beneficial to the company?", "What are your goals?", "What is your biggest accomplishment so far, and disappointment?", "What is your greatest strength, and weakness?", "Describe your work style?", "What motivates you?", "What are you passionate about?", "Are you over qualified for this job?", "What makes you angry?", 'What do you know about this company?", "What are your salary expectations?" etc

- Make your list of questions you want to ask in the interview
- Practice getting your body language right
- Check that you have the correct clothing to wear to the interview and it is clean and ironed
- Find some positive quotes to give yourself confidence

Before the interview

- Make sure you are well groomed and look professional
- Get your CV /Resume, certificates, references etc together and put them in order and into a folder and place them into your clean bag
- Write down the job details, address, interviewers name etc in your notebook that you are going to take with you, and make sure you have a working pen
- Practice your body language again
- Read those positive quotes
- Go to the interview, and think positive confident thoughts on your way. ARRIVE EARLY!!

At the interview

- Make sure you are there at least 10-15 minutes before the scheduled interview time
- Announce yourself at the reception and tell them you are here to meet Mr/Mrs/Miss ...... for a job interview
- Go to the toilet to make sure you are looking good in the mirror
- While sitting and waiting, do some deep breathing to relax into the environment
- Review your personal statements and answers
- Focus on your body language
- When the interviewer comes to meet you, smile, stand up straight and greet them looking straight into their eyes, and if they offer their hand to shake, shake it with a firm grip. (Mirror their greetings and handshake grip)
- Wait for their instructions

In the interview

- Sit down and sit straight upright, place your hands on your lap
- Relax and smile and enjoy the interview, and learn what you can from it
- Listen to the interviewer and keep looking them in the eyes
- Speak clearly and answer the questions as best as possible, remembering what you have prepared
- When asked, or at the end of the interview, ask

if you can ask them some questions, take out your notebook, and read the questions and write down the answers

- Ask the interviewer for their business card (so you can then send them a follow up email)
- When you leave; Stand up straight and smile, say good bye, shake hands again looking them in the eyes, thank them for their time and the interview, turn and walk out with a straight back and head held high

After the interview

- Write down anything you need to remember, what you are feeling and thinking (This will help you for future reference)
- Assess how you felt you did, what you think you did not do well, write it down so you know what you need to improve on
- Write a follow up letter thanking them for their time and the interview, and reminding them of your traits, soft skills and qualities without over doing it! (This is your last chance to make yourself a stand out in their mind that they should hire you!)

6.
TEMPLATES

- Cover Letter

- CV / Resume

- Thank you Letter

The templates provided are to show you a layout. I would suggest you write your own first with all the information you have and from the workbook, then tweak it with ideas from other peoples example. Only put in what applies to you and your skills and abilities. Don't lie or over exaggerate and make sure you know what everything means on these documents. Don't copy something and not know the meaning as you may be asked about it in the interview.

You can go to an internet search engine and type in

- Cover letter examples for (add your degree name) graduate students
- examples of resume for (add your degree name) graduate students

    and look under images, and you can find some examples to tailor make your resume for which ever industry you want to apply for.

Format for a <u>cover letter</u> (USE ONLY 1 A4 page)

Your name and address

Phone number

e-mail

Date

Name (If you don't know the name, call and ask who you should address this letter to)

Address of company

Dear (title and surname of the interviewer)

Add a reference to the job title/position,

(Graduate landscape architecture)

1st paragraph is used for a brief introduction saying who you are, what job you are applying for, where and when you saw the advertisement. Give your university name, degree results if finished, and if still taking the final exams, give expected results. Also state that they can find a CV/Resume attached to the email.

2nd paragraph is used to say why you are interested in the job position and working for that company. Be specific as much as possible.(So you will have to do a bit of research to find out about the company and what they do) Make sure your letter is tailored towards this company (don't send a general letter)

3rd paragraph is used in conjunction with the 2nd paragraph. Here you state why you are a strong candidate for this position adding your strengths, knowledge and skills. Add any experiences and relevant information you have for this particular position, and have references attached to your resume

4th paragraph is used for any other points you would like to express about the job position, such as what you are hoping to gain from the position, and how it matches your career plans. Add any interests and roles of responsibility you have had that is relevant to this position. If you have done anything else that could benefit them, add that here. Example- taking a gap year, or traveling somewhere and explain what you gained from it that can add value to this company.

Conclusion paragraph is used to say you are available for an interview and to start work if accepted. Tell them you look forward to hearing from them. (Keep it short and positive)

Yours sincerely / Yours faithfully (if you don't know the interviewers name)

Sign the letter!

Your name

Format for a <u>Resume</u>

YOUR NAME

Date of Birth:
Your Address: **Optional**
Your City, State, Zip Code: YOUR PHOTO
Your Phone Number:
Your Email Address: (professional email)

PROFILE

Objective: Example - I'm an educated professional looking to align myself with a company, institution or group where I can fully utilize and further develop my skills.

Availability: Currently available

EDUCATION AND QUALIFICATIONS

This paragraph is used to show your degree, the name of your university, when you attended and where the university is located.

If you have done any other courses, you can state them here

University of (Name): A Bachelor of (Science) Degree 2007 – 2013. Name of City and Country

High School: Name of school and address and the years you attended.

Level Attained:

Subjects: English, Maths, Biology, Geography, History etc

ACCOMPLISHMENTS

Here state all the things that you have achieved and accomplished. Anything that you were part of, like a sports team, or social team, your position and what you accomplished.

For example: 1st team football captain

3rd team squash captain

Debating team captain

Use this structure if you have more achievements with results: Three components to use for your achievements

- A particular skill

- A particular activity

- Result and benefits

WORK HISTORY AND EXPERIENCE

If you don't have any work experience, write about any part time work you did, during school or university.

Company:

Dates Employed:

Position:

Duties:

(Make sure you write down everything you did, even if you only did it once, it is something you have done or learnt)

Reasons for Leaving: (State reason)

PROFESSIONAL AND PERSONAL KEY SKILLS AND ABILITIES

This is one of the most important sections to pay attention to for school leavers and University students, as you may not have work experience, so you need to have a good repertoire of skills to get the interviewers attention.

Proficient skills: (Name them)

Languages: (Here state the languages you are proficient, fluent, competent or novice in, speaking, writing and listening)

Example:

English – Proficient Speaking, Writing and Listening

Spanish – Fluent Speaking and Listening

Novice Writing

Chinese – Competent Speaking, Writing and Listening

ACTIVITIES HOBBIES AND INTERESTS

This section is to show what you do when you are not studying or working. Example; what sports you play (are these activities team or individual oriented? They can tell a lot about your personality), debating, photography, running. If you are going to write watching tv, be specific in what programs you watch; example – current news affairs, history channel, national geographic.

Squash, Yoga, Gym, Meditation, Photography, Traveling, Writing books.

REFERENCES ON REQUEST

References can be shown on request.

IN CONCLUSION

A conclusion is not necessary but I like to add one at the end just to leave a personal message for the person reading my resume.

The conclusion should be short and to the point. Display your brand slogan, which skills sums you up as well as your type of character.

This slogan should be truthful and eye/mind catching, so take some time and think about who you are and what your values are and say why they should hire YOU!

*** Please note that by adding a photo it can either limit your chances of getting an interview, or it could play a great role in getting you an interview. It is not necessary to have one on your resume so use discretion in this decision! ***

....

Format for a <u>Thank you letter</u>

Contact Information: *(Here you write your contact information)*
Your Name
Your Address
Your City, State, Zip Code
Your Phone Number
Your Email Address (Make sure you have a professional email address)

Date

Contact Information: *(The interviewers contact details)*
Name
Title
Company
Address
City, State, Zip Code

Greeting:

Dear Mr./Ms. Last Name:

Body of Thank You Letter:

Write your letter in a simple way and keep it focused.

1st paragraph is used to thank the interviewer for their time for interviewing you.

2nd paragraph is used to give reasons why you are the person that should be considered for the position. Here you also list your specific skills that relates to the position of the interview.

3rd paragraph is used for any extra information on your qualifications you had not mentioned in the interview.

Closing paragraph is used for conveying your appreciation for being considered for the open job position and that you look forward to hearing from them soon.

Leave a blank line between each lines below.

Closing:

Best Regards,

Signature:

Handwritten Signature *(If you are sending by normal mail)*

Typed Signature *(If emailing)*

Now you need to ask yourself a few questions in the strategy you want to use in your resume, "Do I want to be a specialist? Or do I want to be a generalist?"

If you know exactly what you are looking for, and have done your research on the company you are applying to, then you can match your skill set to what the company's requirements are, you don't need to add all your skills, only add the skills you think might be useful and compatible. However, if you are not sure, and you are applying for a job where the company has hundreds of employees, then your broad base of skills would be beneficial to the company.

You can also state your primary skills which you are proficient in first, then state your secondary skills which you are competent in. You don't want to congest your resume with unrelated skills, so do your research first before sending your resume.

Tips and early planning

With a lot of early planning, researching and awareness at school level and university level you can find out what is required of you when you enter into the work arena. By doing this, you can improve your chances of getting a great job over and above all the other candidates who are also applying for the same job position.

You need to make yourself employable by having as many soft skills as possible to go with your hard skills. The more activities you do apart from your education, the better, as a future employer can see you are active, and have a lot of other interests, and can see you are a motivated person.

Use the work/mind mapping tool which is powerful and useful in mapping and planning your life. Take this opportunity to learn about it, and start utilizing it in your life! If you are wanting to travel from your house to somewhere, and you don't know the way and you set off to find the place, you will eventually get to that destination, but you may take longer than expected, because you got lost, had to do a u-turn etc and it maybe has cost you a lot of time and money. But if you get a map and plot out the route you need to go in, then you save yourself a lot of time, money and frustration. So this is where the work/mind map will come in good use. Be creative and have fun with it!

7.

Discovering Your Genius:

SKILLS IDENTIFICATION AND GOAL SETTING WORKBOOK

People are hired for their talents, skills and abilities, so get to know all yours.

How many students know what all their skills, strengths and weaknesses are? How many students know their values and personal characteristics? How many students know what their goals are? How students actually know what they want to do in life for a job? Answer: Not many!

A lot of students fail answering these types of questions when going for a job interview, and they stumble at the first hurdle. Let's stop that happening to you!

This workbook has been designed to help you figure out who you are and what your qualities, talents and traits are, in other words, identifying your character and characteristics. It will also help guide you through a step-by-step process in creating goals.

Let's use a technique called **Perceptional Positioning** to help you gain an understanding of what you will go through when going for a job interview. Put yourself in the business owner's positions, as if you were doing the interview and asking the questions to find out about the potential employees talents, skills and abilities.

What would you look for in their cover letter and resume? What questions would you ask them if you invited them to come into your office for an interview? What answers would you be listening and looking out for? What other influencing factors would you be identifying, looking for, or trying to get a feel for?

- Their confidence?

- Their abilities and talents and skill set?

- Their knowledge on the subject?

- Identifying if they are easy to talk to and maybe work with?

- Their appearance?

Before you hire anyone, you would want to have a good feeling about that person you are looking to hire as they will have the responsibility to take your business forward by completing the tasks set out for them to do, and in return you pay them a salary for their contribution to your company! So, ask yourself, "Will this person be of value and be worth that financial return?"
Now you must put yourself back into the interview situation and learn how to answer questions with this understanding.

How to use this workbook!

The more effort and brainstorming you put into doing these exercises, and the more information you dig out of yourself, the more you will surprise yourself at all the resources you have. Once all this becomes clearer you will start to feel more confident in yourself and your abilities.

This is an on-going process, so keep adding and updating your information on these workbook pages. Be creative, and write down everything you can think of. Buy a diary and make it your own "My Genius Book" and let that be your everyday go to book where you are writing down all your "inner jigsaw puzzle pieces" so you can create the picture and dream life you want and bring it into reality.

Have fun but be honest with yourself while doing this workbook! In the end, you will be amazed with yourself and you will see you are worthy!

If you are prepared to give yourself a go, so too will others be prepared to give you a go!

Our Education System

"Everybody is a genius. But if you judge a fish by its ability to climb a tree, it will live its whole life believing that it is stupid."

- Albert Einstein

Every person has a different up-bringing, life experiences, as well as influences from teachers, family and friends. This in turn leads us to all have a different set of talents, skills, qualities and values in which to live life by.

So let's extract these out of you and then you can see what you have to work with. Remember genius, work with what you have and work to your strengths, while working on accumulating more skills while working on changing your negatives and weaknesses to become positives and strengths. Only once you become aware of something, can you do something to enhance it, or change it!

Two of the greatest tools we have at our disposal to use are Awareness and Imagination! Once we become aware of something we don't like, we can use our imagination to change it to our liking.

Enjoy this workbook process while drawing out all your hidden treasures!

Discovering Your Genius:

SKILLS IDENTIFICATION AND GOAL SETTING WORKBOOK

Table of Content:

- Life's satisfaction scorecard - Page 90

Discovering your genius: Understanding yourself and identifying your Core Beliefs:

- IQ vs EQ   Page 96
- Attitude   Page 99
- Self talk   Page 103
- Values   Page 107
- Desires   Page 114
- Qualities / Traits   Page 116
- Talents   Page 128
- Skills   Page 130
- Strengths   Page 143
- Weakness   Page 145
- Passion - Hobbies / Abilities   Page 151
- Goals   Page 156

Let's see how ready you are!

So before you start with this workbook, I want you to give yourself test scores on what you know about the following questions, so you can measure your improvement by the time you have finished this workbook. It is best to be very honest with yourself, and see how much you actually improve by the end of this workbook!

Life's Satisfaction Scorecard

If you were to give yourself a SCORE out of 10.

10 being the best!

"How SATISFIED you are with your life overall?"

1 – 2 – 3 – 4 – 5 – 6 – 7 – 8 – 9 – 10

Rate your Self as being a LEADER!

1 – 2 – 3 – 4 – 5 – 6 – 7 – 8 – 9 – 10

Rate your SELF CONFIDENCE!

1 – 2 – 3 – 4 – 5 – 6 – 7 – 8 – 9 – 10

Rate your SELF DISCIPLINE!

1 – 2 – 3 – 4 – 5 – 6 – 7 – 8 – 9 – 10

How much POWER you think you have in CREATING THE LIFE YOU WANT!

1 – 2 – 3 – 4 – 5 – 6 – 7 – 8 – 9 – 10

"How well you KNOW YOURSELF?" (Self Awareness)

1 – 2 – 3 – 4 – 5 – 6 – 7 – 8 – 9 – 10

KNOWING YOUR SKILLS!

1 – 2 – 3 – 4 – 5 – 6 – 7 – 8 – 9 – 10

KNOWING YOUR QUALITIES, TRAITS and VALUES! (Personality)

1 – 2 – 3 – 4 – 5 – 6 – 7 – 8 – 9 – 10

KNOWING YOUR PERSONAL STRENGTHS!

1 – 2 – 3 – 4 – 5 – 6 – 7 – 8 – 9 – 10

KNOWING YOUR PERSONAL WEAKNESS!

1 – 2 – 3 – 4 – 5 – 6 – 7 – 8 · 9 – 10

KNOWING YOUR STRATEGY FOR SUCCESS!

1 – 2 – 3 – 4 – 5 – 6 – 7 – 8 – 9 – 10

KNOWING HOW TO SET GOALS!

1 – 2 – 3 – 4 – 5 – 6 – 7 – 8 – 9 – 10

KNOWING YOUR PASSION IN LIFE!

1 – 2 – 3 – 4 – 5 – 6 – 7 – 8 – 9 – 10

KNOWING THE DIFFERENCE BETWEEN

IQ and EQ!

1 – 2 – 3 – 4 – 5 – 6 – 7 – 8 – 9 – 10

"How PREPARED are you for a JOB INTERVIEW?"

1 – 2 – 3 – 4 – 5 – 6 – 7 – 8 – 9 – 10

"How confident you are WRITING a cover letter?"

1 – 2 – 3 – 4 – 5 – 6 – 7 – 8 – 9 – 10

"How confident you are in CREATING a Resume?"

1 – 2 – 3 – 4 – 5 – 6 – 7 – 8 – 9 – 10

"How confident are you in GOING FOR A JOB
INTERVIEW?"

1 – 2 – 3 – 4 – 5 – 6 – 7 – 8 – 9 – 10

"How confident you are in GETTING A JOB YOU
DESIRE?"

1 – 2 – 3 – 4 – 5 – 6 – 7 – 8 – 9 – 10

"How much you KNOW WHAT YOU WANT TO DO
IN YOUR LIFE?"

1 – 2 – 3 – 4 – 5 – 6 – 7 – 8 – 9 – 10

Ok, so now you have a rough idea about your Life's Satisfaction scores. Don't worry too much if you didn't score very well on any of the questions, because after you finish the workbook, your scores should be near the 9 to 10 mark, if not, then you may need to go back and look at the areas you didn't do so well at, and see what specifically you can do to change your scores into a 10.

Understanding Yourself and Identifying Your Inner Core Self:

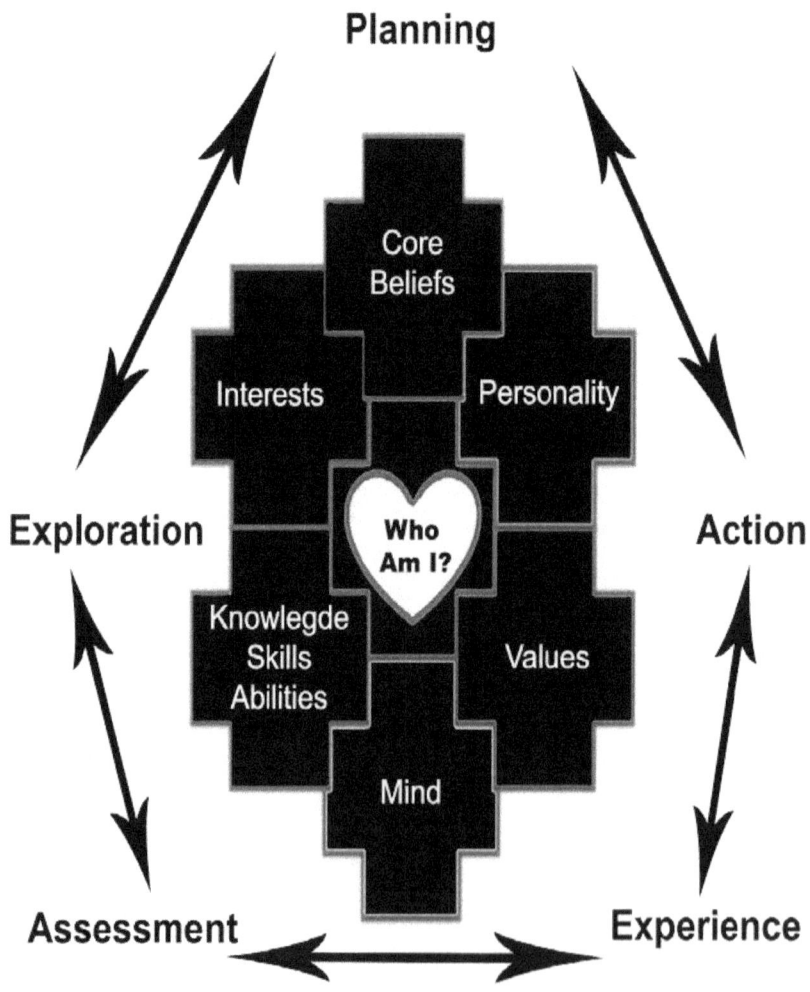

I am also my ...

Mind

Skills

Passion

Qualities / Traits

Desires

Self Talk

Talents

Weakness

Strengths

Goals

WHO AM I?

Before we start, let's have a look at the difference between IQ and EQ so we can see what we are dealing with!

IQ = Intelligence Quotient

EQ = Emotional Quotient (emotional intelligence)

IQ is used to determine academic abilities and identify individuals with off-the-chart intelligence or mental challenges.

"Emotional Intelligence, or emotional quotient (EQ), is defined as an individual's ability to identify, evaluate, control, and express emotions. People with high EQ usually make great leaders and team players because of their ability to understand, empathize, and connect with the people around them. IQ, or intelligence quotient, is score derived from standardized testing designed to assess an individual's intelligence.

EQ is a better indicator of success in the workplace and is used to identify leaders, good team players, and people who work best by themselves.

What is EQ?

According to the University of New Hampshire psychology department, emotional intelligence is the "ability to validly reason with emotions and to use emotions to enhance thought." EQ refers to an individual's ability to perceive, control, evaluate, and express emotions.

People with high EQ can manage emotions, use their emotions to facilitate thinking, understand emotional meanings and accurately perceive others' emotions. EQ is partially determined by how a person relates to others and maintains emotional control.

What is IQ?

Intelligence quotient or IQ is a score received from standardized assessments designed to test intelligence. IQ relates directly to intellectual pursuits such as the ability to learn as well as understand and apply information to skill sets. IQ covers logical reasoning, word comprehension and math skills. People with higher IQ can think in abstracts and make connections by making generalizations easier.

There are differing perspectives on whether EQ or IQ is more important. Those in the EQ camp say "A high IQ will get you through school, a high EQ will get you through life." - Diffen

Definition:

- ☐ Emotional quotient (EQ) or emotional intelligence is the ability to identify, assess, and control the emotions of oneself, of others, and of groups.

- ☐ An intelligence quotient (IQ) is a score derived from one of several standardized tests designed to assess intelligence.

Abilities:

☐ EQ: Identify, evaluate, control and express emotions one's own emotions; perceive, and assess others' emotions; use emotions to facilitate thinking, understand emotional meanings.

☐ IQ: Ability to learn, understand and apply information to skills, logical reasoning, word comprehension, math skills, abstract and spatial thinking, filter irrelevant information.

In the workplace:

☐ EQ: Teamwork, leadership, successful relations, service orientation, initiative, collaboration.

☐ IQ: Success with challenging tasks, ability to analyze and connect the dots, research and development.

Identifies:

☐ EQ: Leaders, team-players, individuals who best work alone, individuals with social challenges.

☐ IQ: Highly capable or gifted individuals, individuals with mental challenges and special needs.

☐

Core Beliefs: Attitude

Your Attitude is KEY to success!

Mental Attitude

Q. What is attitude?

A. Attitude is a feeling or way of thinking that affects a person's behavior the way a person views something or tends to behave towards it, often in an evaluative way (determine the worth / significance)

- a feeling or way of thinking that affects a person's behavior

Q. What is a positive attitude?

A. A positive attitude is a philosophy of approaching life with optimism and confidence. (Optimism - a feeling or belief that good things will happen in the future : a feeling or belief that what you hope for will happen)

Significance and effect of a Positive Attitude!

Significance: Your attitude can determine your success or failure in your career and relationships. Putting forth positive energy is more likely to get you positive results, while negative energy is likely to cause problems.

Effects: Having a positive attitude can translate into a new outlook on life by enabling a person to gain power over his thoughts and emotions, thus changing his outlook on life.

A + attitude is everything.

Both + and – thoughts, views and feelings ARE equally powerful!

What is your attitude like NOW? How do you see yourself at this moment? Be specific!

....

....

....

....

....

....

....

....

....

....

....

....

....

....

Developing a positive attitude requires replacing negative thinking with positive thinking in an effort to create a successful outlook on life!

How do you want to see yourself? Describe the attitude you want to work with from NOW ON!

Be specific!

....
....
....
....
....
....
....
....
....
....
....
....
....
....
....
....
....
....

Specific = Clear and detailed in communicating

☐ "I AM"

☐ **Two of the most POWERFUL words. For what you put after them, shapes your reality! Affirmations are a great way to practice positive and uplifting self talk!**

☐ "I am what I think!"

☐ "I am what I do!"

☐ "I am what I eat and drink!"

☐ "I am successful!"

☐ "I am a winner!"

☐ "I am ………………………………………….!"
(add your own list)

☐ "I am ………………………………………….!"

☐ "I am ………………………………………….!"

☐ "I am ………………………………………….!"

☐ "I am ………………………………………….!"

☐ "I am ………………………………………….!"

☐ "I am ………………………………………….!"

☐ "I am ………………………………………….!"

SELF-TALK

Definition:

- the act or practice of talking to oneself, either aloud or silently and mentally

Self-Talk is the single most important function that you **MUST** become aware of.

WHAT ARE YOU THINKING AND SAYING TO YOURSELF?

What you say and think to yourself <u>WILL</u> determine your outcome in life, as the internal manifests the external.

<u>I CANNOT STATE THIS STRONGLY ENOUGH!!!</u>

A great way to become aware of what you are thinking and saying to yourself is through the Art of Meditation, which will not only "highlight" what you are thinking, but can also bring you into a state of peace and mindfulness which will help you cope with any outside circumstances and obstacles.

If your self-talk is not positive, then you need to work on changing that as your Number 1 Priority!

Write your list of NEGATIVE things you say to yourself:
(negative and bad) Be truthful, and be as specific as you can
be!

Negatives:...

....

....

....

....

....

....

....

....

....

....

....

....

....

....

....

....

....

....

....

**Only once you become aware of what you are saying
to yourself can you change the energy pattern into a
positive energy pattern.**

Write your list of POSITIVE and GOOD things you say to yourself. (Positive and good)

Positives:………………………………………………………
………………………………………………………………………
………………………………………………………………………
………………………………………………………………………
………………………………………………………………………
………………………………………………………………………
………………………………………………………………………
………………………………………………………………………
………………………………………………………………………
………………………………………………………………………
………………………………………………………………………
………………………………………………………………………
………………………………………………………………………
………………………………………………………………………
………………………………………………………………………
………………………………………………………………………
………………………………………………………………………
………………………………………………………………………
………………………………………………………………………
………………………………………………………………………
………………………………………………………………………
………………………………………………………………………
………………………………………………………………………
………………………………………………………………………
………………………………………………………………………
………………………………………………………………………
………………………………………………………………………

Now compare the Positives VS the Negatives! Which ones are you going to start paying attention to?

Now take the NEGATIVE and BAD things you have written down and use a REFRAME TECHNIQUE to change them into positives. Take the negatives and reframe them into POSITIVES in a way that will work for you. When you change the meaning by putting it into a different context, setting or frame, this changes the meaning which then changes our responses and behaviours.

....

....

....

....

....

....

....

....

....

....

....

....

....

....

....

....

....

....

VALUES

Definition:

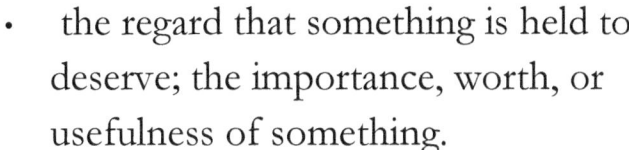

- the regard that something is held to deserve; the importance, worth, or usefulness of something.

- a person's principles or standards of behavior; one's judgment of what is important in life.

- Your Values are what is important to you in life. Knowing your Values helps you understand what drives you – what you enjoy, inspires you and would like more of. By building a life and lifestyle around our values we create a life that is more satisfying and meaningful to us.

- NB. Values change over time, and deepen as you understand yourself better – they are always moving. Your Values can also be situational - so what is true for you at work may not be true for you at home.

- Finally, the Values "'List" below is ONLY to give you some ideas of example or sample values. We are each unique, so there will undoubtedly be words that are missing from this list, and different words that sum up your Values better. Feel free to add words to the list below.

- Remember: When it comes to Values, there is no right or wrong – only who WE are!

"Great Values are built on strong moral foundations. Men become great when they allow these values to take root within their souls and live by them!"
– Lincoln Patz

"There is no value in doubting yourself. Accept your brilliance!
– Mo Ali

✓ Tick the values which identify you, and add others if you don't see them here!

- Accessibility
- Accomplishment
- Accountability
- Accuracy
- Achievement
- Acknowledgement
- Activeness
- Adaptability
- Advancement
- Adventure
- Affection
- Agility
- Ambition
- Anticipation
- Appreciation
- Approachability
- Attractiveness
- Authenticity
- Availability
- Awareness
- Balance
- Beauty
- Being the best
- Benevolence
- Boldness
- Bravery
- Calm
- Capability
- Care

- Challenge
- Change
- Cheerfulness
- Clarity
- Collaboration
- Commitment
- Community
- Compassion
- Competence
- Composure
- Comradeship
- Concentration
- Confidence
- Congruency
- Connectedness
- Consistency
- Contentment
- Contribution
- Cooperation
- Cooperation
- Courage
- Courage
- Courtesy
- Creativity
- Credibility
- Curiosity
- Depth
- Desire
- Determination

- Devotion
- Dignity
- Diligence
- Directness
- Discipline
- Discovery
- Discretion
- Drive
- Duty
- Dynamism
- Ease
- Education
- Effectiveness
- Efficiency
- Effortlessness
- Elegance
- Empathy
- Empowerment
- Encouragement
- Endurance
- Enjoyment
- Entertainment
- Enthusiasm
- Environment
- Environmentalism
- Ethics
- Excellence
- Excitement
- Experience
- Exploration
- Expressiveness
- Fairness
- Financial independence
- Firmness
- Fitness
- Flexibility
- Fluency
- Focus
- Forgiveness
- Freedom
- Friendship
- Frugality
- Fun
- Generosity
- Gentleness
- Giving
- Gratitude
- Grounded
- Growth
- Guidance
- Happiness
- Harmony
- Health
- Helpfulness
- Honesty
- Honour
- Hospitality
- Humility
- Humour
- Hygiene
- Idealism
- Imagination
- Independence
- Individuality

- Influence
- Ingenuity
- Innovation
- Inquisitiveness
- Insightfulness
- Inspiration
- Integrity
- Intellect
- Intelligence
- Introspection
- Intuition
- Intuitiveness
- Investing
- Involvement
- Joy
- Kindness
- Knowledge
- Leadership
- Learning
- Listening
- Logic
- Love
- Loyalty
- Making a difference
- Mastery
- Meticulousness
- Mindfulness
- Modesty
- Motivation
- Mysteriousness
- Open-mindedness
- Openness
- Optimism

- Orderliness
- Organization
- Originality
- Outdoors
- Participation
- Partnership
- Passion
- Patience
- Peace
- Perceptiveness
- Perfection
- Perseverance
- Persuasiveness
- Philanthropy
- Pragmatism
- Precision
- Preparedness
- Presence
- Pride
- Privacy
- Proactively
- Productivity
- Professionalism
- Prosperity
- Punctuality
- Recognition
- Recreation
- Refinement
- Reflection
- Relaxation
- Reliability
- Religiousness
- Reputation

- Resilience
- Resolution
- Resolve
- Resourcefulness
- Respect
- Responsibility
- Reverence
- Romance
- Sacredness
- Sacrifice
- Safety
- Saintliness
- Satisfaction
- Self-control
- Self-Esteem
- Selflessness
- Self-reliance
- Self-respect
- Sensitivity
- Sensuality
- Serenity
- Service
- Sexuality
- Sharing
- Significance
- Silence
- Silliness
- Simplicity
- Skillfulness
- Solidarity
- Solitude
- Sophistication
- Spirit
- Spirituality
- Spontaneity
- Stability
- Status
- Stealth
- Stillness
- Strength
- Structure
- Success
- Support
- Sympathy
- Synergy
- Tact
- Teaching
- Teamwork
- Temperance
- Thankfulness
- Thoroughness
- Thoughtfulness
- Tidiness
- Tolerance
- Tradition
- Tranquility
- Transcendence
- Trust
- Truth
- Understanding
- Uniqueness
- Unity
- Usefulness
- Valor
- Vigor
- Virtue

- o Vision
- o Vitality
- o Volunteering
- o Wealth
- o Willfulness
- o Willingness
- o Winning
- o Wisdom

Make a list of your top 20, and be specific why these are your top values!

1...
2...
3...
4...
5...
6...
7...
8...
9...
10..
11..
12..
13..
14..
15..
16..
17..
18..
19..
20..

DESIRES

Definition:

- to want or wish for (something)

What is it that you truly desire, or wish for?

You have many realms to work in:

- Physical life – job, house, car, security etc

- Emotional life – feelings, joy, happiness, love etc

- Spiritual life – connection to the Great Spirit and yourself

- Intellectual life – thoughts, the way you think life

Life is a Step – by - Step Process on every level, (job, relationship, thought patterns, actions, emotions etc) and where you put your next step matters and affects your life!

Sometimes you have to place your steps where you don't want to, and that's ok!

Just be mindful of what you want, and use those steps as stepping stones to get you back to where you want to be!

Make your list of all your passions:

....

....

....

....

....

....

....

....

....

....

....

....

....

....

....

....

....

....

....

QUALITIES / TRAITS

Definition: Qualities

- the standard of something as measured against other things of a similar kind; the degree of excellence of something.

- a distinctive attribute or characteristic possessed by someone

Definition: Traits

- a distinguishing characteristic or quality, especially of one's personal nature

- is something about you that makes you "you."

> **"What is it that**
>
> **SETS YOU APART**
>
> **from others?"**

Understanding your personality

Definition of personality –

- the combination of characteristics or qualities that form an individual's distinctive character

- the set of emotional qualities, ways of behaving, etc., that makes a person different from other people

- attractive qualities (such as energy, friendliness, and humor) that make a person interesting or pleasant to be with

- attractive qualities that make something unusual or interesting

- the complex of characteristics that distinguishes an individual: the totality of an individual's behavioral and emotional characteristics

- a set of distinctive traits and characteristics

- distinction or excellence of personal and social traits

Totality of an individual's behavioral and emotional characteristics. Personality embraces a person's moods, attitudes, opinions, motivations, and style of thinking, perceiving, speaking, and acting. It is part of what makes each individual distinct.

Qualities and Traits are your Actions, Attitudes and Behaviors

Some Positive personality traits:

✓ Tick the positive personality traits which identify you.

- Able
- Accommodating
- Accurate
- Active
- **Adventurous**
- Affectionate
- Agreeable
- Ambitious
- Amusing
- Analytical
- Appreciative
- Articulate
- Artistic
- Assertive
- Attentive
- Authentic
- Balanced
- Bright
- Brilliant
- Calm
- **Capable**
- Careful
- Caring
- Casual
- Cautious
- Changeable
- **Charming**
- Cheerful
- Clean
- Clear-Headed
- Clever
- Clownish
- Comical
- Communicative
- Compassionate
- Competent
- Composed
- **Confident**
- **Conscientious**
- Considerate
- Consistent
- Constructive
- Cool-Headed
- Cooperative
- Cordial
- Courageous
- Courteous
- Creative
- **Cultured**
- Curious
- Daredevil
- Decent
- Decisive
- **Dependable**
- Dignified
- Diligent

- Diplomatic
- Direct
- Disciplined
- Discreet
- Dutiful
- Eager
- Easy going
- Eccentric
- Educated
- Effective
- Encouraging
- Energetic
- Enterprising
- Entertaining
- Enthusiastic
- Ethical
- Excitable
- Excited
- Experienced
- Extroverted
- Exuberant
- Fair
- Fashionable
- Fault-Finding
- Fearless
- Flexible
- Forgiving
- Forthright
- Forward
- Frank
- Friendly
- Generous

- Gentle
- Genuine
- Good
- Good-Humored
- Good-Natured
- Good-Tempered
- Graceful
- Gracious
- Growing
- Happy
- Hard working
- Hard-Hearted
- Helpful
- High-Spirited
- Honest
- Honorable
- Hopeful
- Humble
- Humorous
- Imaginative
- Impartial
- Independent
- Individualistic
- Industrious
- Inquisitive
- Insightful
- Intellectual
- Intelligent
- Interesting
- Intolerant
- Intuitive
- Inventive

- Keen
- Kind
- Kind-Hearted
- Kindly
- Level-Headed
- Light-Hearted
- Likable
- Literary
- Lively
- Logical
- Loyal
- Lucky
- Mathematical
- Mature
- Meditative
- Meek
- Melancholy
- Methodical
- **Meticulous**
- Moral
- Moralistic
- Neat
- Nice
- **Obedient**
- Objective
- Obliging
- **Observant**
- Open-Minded
- Opinionated
- Opportunist
- **Optimistic**
- Orderly
- Original
- Outgoing
- Outspoken
- Outstanding
- Passive
- Patient
- Perceptive
- Perfectionist
- **Persistent**
- Persuasive
- Philosophical
- Pleasant
- Poised
- Polite
- Popular
- Positive
- Possessive
- Practical
- **Precise**
- Productive
- Proficient
- Progressive
- Prompt
- Proud
- Prudent
- Punctual
- Purposeful
- Quick
- Quick-Witted
- Quiet

- Radical
- Rational
- Realist
- Realistic
- Reasonable
- Refined
- Relaxed
- **Reliable**
- Resourceful
- Respectable
- Respectful
- Responsible
- Romantic
- Scientific
- Self-Assured
- Self-Confident
- Self-Controlled
- Self-Critical
- Self-Disciplined
- Self-Reliant
- Self-Sufficient
- Sensible
- Sensitive
- Sentimental
- Sharp-Witted
- Sincere
- Skilled
- Skillful
- Smart
- Sociable
- Social
- Soft-Hearted
- Soft-Spoken
- Solemn
- Sophisticated
- Spirited
- Sportsmanlike
- Stern
- Strong-Minded
- Subtle
- Sympathetic
- Systematic
- Tactful
- Talented
- Talkative
- Theatrical
- Thorough
- Thoughtful
- Tidy
- Tolerant
- Tough
- Trustful
- **Trusting**
- Trustworthy
- Truthful
- Understanding
- **Valiant**
- Versatile
- Vigorous
- Vivacious
- Warm
- Warm-Hearted
- Well-Mannered
- Well-Read

- o Well-Spoken
- o Wholesome

- o Wise
- o Witty

Make your list of your top 15 positive qualities / traits:

1...
2...
3...
4...
5...
6...
7...
8...
9...
10..
11..
12..
13..
14..
15..

Then choose your top 5 that you can use in your resume!

1...
2...
3...
4...
5...

Notes:

....
....
....
....
....
....
....
....
....
....
....
....
....
....
....
....
....
....
....
....
....
....
....
....
....
....

Some Negative personality traits:

✓ Tick the negative personality traits which identify you.

o Absent-Minded	o Disturbed
o Abusive	o Dominating
o Aggressive	o Domineering
o Aimless	o Dull
o Angry	o Egotistical
o Annoying	o Envious
o Antisocial	o Fault-Finding
o Anxious	o Finicky
o Argumentative	o Foolish
o Arrogant	o Forgetful
o Boring	o Frustrated
o Bossy	o Gossipy
o Childish	o Greedy
o Complaining	o Grouchy
o Conceited	o Helpless
o Cowardly	o Hostile
o Cynical	o Hot-Headed
o Deceptive	o Hot-Tempered
o Depressed	o Ill-Mannered
o Dishonest	o Illogical
o Dishonesty	o Ill-Tempered
o Dishonorable	o Impolite
o Dislikable	o Impractical
o Disobedient	o Impulsive
o Disrespectful	o Inaccurate
o Dissatisfied	o Inattentive
o Distrustful	o Incompetent

- Inconsistent
- Indecisive
- Indifferent
- Inefficient
- Insecure
- Insincere
- Insolent
- Insulting
- Intolerant
- Irresponsible
- Irritable
- Irritating
- Jealous
- Jumpy
- Laziness
- Lazy
- Liar
- Lonely
- Lonesome
- Loud-Mouthed
- Malicious
- Mean
- Meddlesome
- Messy
- Moody
- Narrow-Minded
- Neglectful
- Negligent
- Nervous
- Neurotic
- Obnoxious
- Offensive

- Pessimistic
- Phony
- Picky
- Pompous
- Quarrelsome
- Rebellious
- Reckless
- Resentful
- Restless
- Rude
- Sad
- Sarcastic
- Scornful
- Self-Centred
- Selfish
- Short-Tempered
- Skeptical
- Sneaky
- Snobbish
- Spiteful
- Stingy
- Stubborn
- Surly
- Tactless
- Thoughtless
- Troublesome
- Unappealing
- Unappreciative
- Uncivil
- Unentertaining
- Unenthusiastic
- Unethical

- o Unforgiving
- o **Unfriendly**
- o Ungraceful
- o Ungracious
- o Ungrateful
- o Unhappy
- o Unhealthy
- o Unimaginative
- o Un-industrious
- o Un-inquisitive
- o Uninspiring
- o Uninteresting
- o Unkind
- o Unkindly
- o Unobservant
- o Unoriginal
- o Unpleasant
- o Unpleasing
- o Unpopular
- o Unpredictable
- o Unproductive
- o Unpunctual
- o Unreasonable
- o Unreliable
- o Unromantic
- o **Unruly**
- o Unskilled
- o Unsociable
- o Unsophisticated
- o Unsporting
- o Unsportsmanlike
- o Unsympathetic
- o Untidy
- o Untiring
- o Untrustworthy
- o Untruthful
- o Unwise
- o Vain
- o **Vulgar**
- o Wasteful
- o Weak
- o Withdrawing
- o Withdrawn
- o Worrier

Once you have identified your negative traits, you can list the ones you want to change into positive ones.

Then ask yourself "What specifically do I have to do to change these negative traits into positive traits?" "And for what purpose do I want to change these negative traits into positive traits?"

....

....

....

....

....

....

....

....

....

....

....

....

....

....

....

....

....

....

....

....

....

....

....

TALENTS

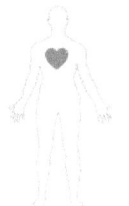

Definition:

- a special ability that allows someone to do something well

- a special, often creative natural ability or aptitude

- a person or persons with special ability,

- especially in a particular field

- a natural ability to excel at a duty or action

Think back on your life, and is there anything other people told you that you are really good at or talented at.

Write down all answers that come to you no matter how small, or silly or inconsequential they may be or seem.

- Is anything here unique, or unusual that you can do and do well?

- What comes easily to you?

- What things are you drawn to and you can do with little effort?

Make your list of all your talents:

. . . .

. . . .

. . . .

. . . .

. . . .

. . . .

. . . .

. . . .

. . . .

. . . .

Take your best talents and describe them in great detail and be specific: Why? What? Who? When? Where? How?

. . . .

. . . .

. . . .

. . . .

. . . .

. . . .

. . . .

. . . .

. . . .

. . . .

. . . .

. . . .

SKILLS

Definition:

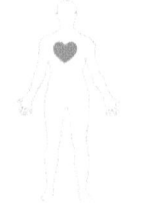

- proficiency, facility, or dexterity that is acquired or developed through training or experience (an ability to do or learn something well and easily, skill in performing tasks, especially with the hands)

Our Skill Set is what makes us all different!

WHAT MAKES US ALL DIFFERENT? OUR SKILLS SET!

Types of skills you will need to succeed:

- Hard skills

- Soft skills

- Personal / Interpersonal skills

- Skills employers are looking for

- Transferable work skills

- Management skills

- Leadership skills

- Entrepreneur Skills

What are Skills?

- A skill is a learned ability

Personal Skills:

- The ability to communicate effectively with people in a friendly way, in a social and business environment.

Hard Skills:

- Skills relating to a specific task or situation. These skills are easily quantifiable.

Soft Skills:

- Personality traits, social graces, communication, personal habits, friendliness, and optimism that characterize relationships with other people.

Life Skills:

- A set of human skills acquired via learning or direct experience that are used to handle problems and questions commonly encountered in daily human life

Business Skills:

- An ability and capacity acquired through deliberate, systematic, and sustained effort to smoothly and adaptively carryout complex activities or job functions involving ideas (cognitive skills), things (technical skills), and/or people (interpersonal skills).

HARD SKILLS

Definition:

- Hard skills are specific, teachable abilities that may be required in a given context, such as a job or university application

- Specific, teachable abilities that can be defined and measured.

Hard skills include job skills like typing, writing, math, reading and the ability to use software programs . Something measurable!

So what are hard skills? Hard skill are your theoretical learnt abilities, your education and your experiences you have gained/achieved, which is brain powered. These skills can be measured. Some examples:

✓ Tick the hard skills which identify you!

  o A Degree or Certificates

  o Accounting

  o Bookkeeping

  o Chemistry

  o Copywriting

  o Finance

  o Graphic Design

  o Language Proficiency

  o Mathematics

  o Programming

  o Machine operation

  o Statistics

  o Some type of development

  o Some type of management

  o Using word, excel, power point, photoshop etc

  o Typing / taking minutes at meetings

  o ....

  o ....

SOFT SKILLS

Definition:

• Soft Skills are Personal attributes that enable someone to interact effectively and harmoniously with other people.

• Term often associated with a person's "EQ" (Emotional Intelligence Quotient)

Soft skills have more to do with who we are than what we know. As such, soft skills encompass the character traits that decide how well one interacts with others, and are usually a definite part of one's personality.

Soft Skills / People Skills / Interpersonal Skills

School leavers and graduated university students may or may not have the practical experience of using their hard skills in the work place yet, therefore they need to compensate that by having a large range (a stock of skills or types of behaviour that a person habitually uses) of soft skills / people skills which they can bring to the interviewers attention. This is where being "street wise" can help you a lot!

So, what are soft skills? Soft skills are not really learnt at school, but in your everyday environment.

If you pay attention to what is going on around you, everything can become a great teacher to you, and you can pick up some great soft skills, good habits and great personal touches by watching other people in action. Become a people watcher to see what they are doing and saying, and if they are good qualities, add them to your character, if you see or feel any that are not good, look inside yourself to see if you have those negative qualities, and work on getting rid of them!

These skills cannot really be measured, they are subjective skills. These are the skills in which you relate to others, or people skills. Some examples"

✓ Tick the soft skills which identify you!

o Adaptable

o Ambitious

o Analytical

o Articulate

o Caring

o Competitive

o Dedicated

o Dependable

o Detail oriented

o Empathy

o Exceeding expectations

o Flexibility

o Focused

- Goal oriented
- Good at achieving results
- Great communication
- Honest
- Humour
- Integrity
- Intuitive
- Motivation

- Negotiation
- Organized
- Passionate
- Patience
- Team work
- Technically minded
- Time management
- ....
- ....

PERSONAL SKILLS

Definition:

- Ability to interact positively and work effectively with others.

Interpersonal skills :

- Is the ability to get along with others while getting the job done. Interpersonal skills include everything from communication and listening skills to attitude and deportment as well as delegation of tasks and leadership. (behaves and stands)

- Good interpersonal skills are a prerequisite for many positions in an organization.

- Works well with others, sensitive, supportive, motivates others, shares the credit, cooperates, delegates effectively, represents others, understands feelings, self confident, and accepts responsibility

SKILLS EMPLOYERS WANT

Top Skills/Qualities Employers Look For:

✓ Tick the skills which you have!

- o Ability making decisions and problem-solving skill

- o Ability to obtain and process information

- o Ability to plan, organize and prioritize work

- o Ability to sell and influence others

- o Ability to work in a team

- o Analytical/quantitative skill

- o Communication skills (verbal)

- o Communication skills (written)

- o Computer skills

o Creativity

o Detail-oriented

o Entrepreneurial skills/risk-taker

o Flexibility/adaptability

o Friendly/outgoing personality

o Initiative

o Interpersonal skills

o Leadership

o Organizational ability

o Strategic planning skill

o Strong work ethic

o Tactfulness

o Technical knowledge skills relating to the job

TRANSFERABLE SKILLS

All the skills you have acquired through experiences from your school, university, work , hobbies, daily living etc

As you start your working career, you should try and learn as much as possible about everything you possibly can, open your eyes, ears and mind to how things are done, as these are the skills that you take with you when you leave your job, and take with you in getting another, better and higher paying job, which can in turn give you the required skill set to open your own business, or take you to the top of a company.

❖ Work smart as you go!

❖ You can never know too much!

❖ Skills are what set us all apart!

Make your list of your top transferable skills:

1..

2..

3..

4..

5..

6..

7..

8..

9..

10...

11...

12...

13...

14...

15...

16...

17...

18...

19...

20...

MANAGEMENT SKILLS

The reason I have added this section is for you to have something to work towards!

The ability to make business decisions and lead subordinates (workers) within a company.

Three most common skills include:

1) Human skills - the ability to interact and motivate

2) Technical skills – the knowledge and proficiency in trade

3) Vision and conceptual skills - the ability to understand concepts and develop these ideas and implement strategies with a great ability in communication and negotiating tactics.

LEADERSHIP SKILLS

Leadership has been described as "a process of social influence in which a person can enlist the aid and support of others in the accomplishment of a common tasks". For example, some understand a leader simply as somebody whom people follow, or as somebody who guides or directs others, while others define leadership as "organizing a group of people to achieve a common goal"

Studies of leadership have produced theories involving traits, situational interaction, function,
behavior, power ,vision and values, charisma, and intelligence, among others.

From Wikipedia, the free encyclopedia

Skills that are likely to be relevant to a wide variety of leadership positions and situations

✓ Tick the Leadership Skills you have!

- Accountable
- Advising
- Ambition
- Authentic
- Available
- Calculating
- Coaching
- Collaborating
- Collaborative
- Committed

- Communicating
- Compassionate
- Confidence
- Coordinating
- Creating
- Credible
- Delegating
- Designing
- Empathic
- Enthusiastic

- Equitable
- Ethical
- Evaluating
- Explaining
- Humble
- Initiating
- Inspirational
- Integrity
- Knowledgeable – about self and others
- Motivating
- Motivation Skills
- Motivational
- Negotiating
- Networking
- Optimistic
- Partnering
- Passionate
- People Skills
- Persistent
- Planning
- Problem solving
- Producing
- Proving
- Referring
- Reliable
- Resilient
- Resolving
- Resourceful
- Respectful
- Responsibility
- Summarizing
- Supervising
- Trustworthy
- Vision
- Visionary

STRENGTHS AND WEAKNESS

Definition: Strength

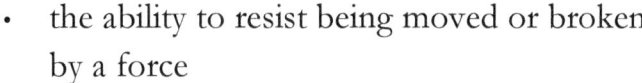

- the ability to resist being moved or broken by a force

- the quality that allows someone to deal with problems in a determined and effective way

- the state or quality of being physically or <u>mentally</u>

strong

"What is a strength? A strength is the ability to consistently provide near-perfect performance in a specific activity. The key to building a strength is to identify your dominant talents, then complement them by acquiring knowledge and skills pertinent to the activity." - Gallup

By knowing your top strengths, you have something to work with, and knowing your top weaknesses, you have something to work on.

Some positive personality traits:

✓ Tick your personality strengths!

- o Accurate
- o Ambitious

- o Adventurous
- o Appreciative

- Caring
- Compassionate
- Considerate
- Courageous
- Creative
- Dedicated
- Determined
- Disciplined
- Educated
- Enthusiastic
- Forceful
- Friendly
- Generous
- Good looking
- Helpful
- Honest
- Humorous
- Idealistic
- Independent
- Inspiring
- Intelligent
- Intuitive
- Leadership
- Lively
- Logical
- Observant
- Open
- Open-Minded
- Optimistic
- Orderly
- Organized
- Patient
- People skills
- Persuasive
- Practical
- Respectful
- Responsible
- Self controlled

o Self-assured   o Tolerant

o Serious   o Trust Worthy

o Speaking   o Trustworthy

o Spontaneous   o Versatile

o Straightforward   o Warm

o Tactful   o Willpower

o Thoughtful

WEAKNESS

Definition: Weakness

- Lacking physical strength, energy, or vigor

- Lacking aptitude or skill

- Lacking or resulting from a lack of intelligence.

- Lacking persuasiveness; unconvincing

- Lacking authority or the power to govern
  Lacking potency or intensity:

What are your weaknesses?

Once you identify your weaknesses, you can then make a plan on working on them to change them into strengths, adding more tools to your toolbox.

Some weakness personality traits:

✓ Tick your personality weaknesses!

o Aggressive	o Hard
o Arrogant	o Impatient
o Blunt	o Indifferent
o Bossy	o Inflexible
o Chaotic	o Inhibited
o Complaining	o Intolerant
o Contemptuous	o Lazy
o Cynical	o Loose-tongued
o Dull	o Mistrustful
o Fanatical	o Moody
o Fearful	o Naive
o Greedy	o Obstructive

o Passive	o Shy
o Prejudiced	o Sloppy
o Pushy	o Stand-offish
o Reckless	o Strict
o Rude	o Stubborn
o Selfish	o Undisciplined
o Shallow	o Vague
o Short-sighted	o Wasteful

"Sometimes our Greatest Strength comes from our Greatest Weakness,

So knowing your Weaknesses are just as important as knowing your Strengths!"

List Your Top Strengths and Weaknesses

Strengths: Be specific why they are your strengths.

1..

....

2..

....

3..

....

4..

....

5..

....

6..

....

7..

....

8..

....

9..

....

10..

....

Weaknesses: Be specific why they are your weaknesses.

1..

....

2..

....

3..

....

4..

....

5..

....

6..

....

7..

....

8..

....

9..

....

10..

....

My Skill Set

My Occupation..

SKILLS I HAVE	SKILLS I NEED TO WORK ON	SKILLS I NEED

Your Passion: Hobbies – Talents – Abilities

Why am I putting this into a job interview book? Well you may not want to work for someone your whole life, and this can help you by giving you something to work towards once you have got a job, and you are getting a salary which you can use to put towards your own business or project.

OR, if you want to work for yourself and not someone else, and you are not sure what to do.

Make a list identifying all your hobbies, talents and abilities and see how you can mold them together and monetize them.

List all the things you can do in all areas of your life, from daily living, social, work, education, sport etc. Once they are all written down, you can get a clear picture on how to piece them together. It is like your own jigsaw puzzle, and you are reveling your pieces, then putting them together to create your own picture. So don't leave anything out no matter how small, large, significant or even insignificant it may seem. Brain storm and then let all the pieces come together.

Living your passion, your dream!

Hobbies = YOUR PASSION AND INTERESTS: **ALL** the things you love doing in your free time. What gives you energy, and doesn't feel like work, and you can easily jump out of bed and go and do it!

<u>My Hobbies</u>

....

....

....

....

....

....

....

....

....

....

....

....

....

....

....

....

....

....

....

....

....

Talents = Things you are very good at doing naturally.

<u>My Talents</u>

....

....

....

....

....

....

....

....

....

....

....

....

....

....

....

....

....

....

....

Abilities = Things you can do. (Maybe you have only done the activity once, but understand what is required to do it again.) Write as many things down as possible, no matter how large or small or insignificant you think it may be, just write it down. You can split this into different sections; Hobbies, Social, Work etc

<u>My Abilities</u>

. . . .

. . . .

. . . .

. . . .

. . . .

. . . .

. . . .

. . . .

. . . .

. . . .

. . . .

. . . .

. . . .

. . . .

. . . .

. . . .

. . . .
. . . .
. . . .
. . . .
. . . .
. . . .
. . . .
. . . .
. . . .
. . . .
. . . .
. . . .
. . . .
. . . .
. . . .

Now take the pieces from each section, brainstorm on them and do your research and see if there is a market for them, then see how you can join them all together and create a system to turn them into a living and make money from them. Don't let the money be the main focus, let the money flow to you by being passionate about the action you are doing.

The next section is on goals, goal setting and how to follow them through to success.

GOALS

Definition:

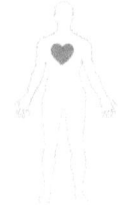

- the object of a person's ambition or effort; an aim or desired result

Why set goals? Why is making a list of things you want to do important?

Goal setting is a great way to focus on what you want to achieve, and the steps needed to be taken to reach this goal or target.

It also helps you take control of your life, you become more focused on what is important right now and you place a time factor to work within to achieve the results you want. It is creating a road map of where you are now, and plotting out the journey you need to take to get to your desired destination.

Example: If you are in city A and you want to go to city B, however you don't know the way or how to get there. Would it not be easier to get hold of a map to see the direction in which you need to go in, rather than just setting off in a direction not knowing where you are going?

Yes, you may end up in city B after some time or

even after a long time, and yes maybe the trip is good and eventful, but it would be just as eventful, a lot quicker and you can get to see and do a lot more if you had a "MAP" to show you the way.

Goal setting and "MIND MAPPING" is a way for you to plan your journey, which includes knowing which road to take, identifying what you want to see and experience along the way, identifying the places you want to go to in order to gain some kind of experience.

It also helps you identify all the option available to you. Do you fly, take a train or go slowly on all the back roads if you don't want to go fast by driving on the highway!

Write down your IDEA – PLAN what action you need to take – IMPLEMENT the Steps one by one – Persevere until you achieve the SUCCESS you want!

It is all in the journey and not the destination that truly matters, it's the step – by –step process which you gain the most from, so be open to all possibilities.

"People with clear, written goals, accomplish far more in a shorter period of time than people without them could ever imagine!"

Goals = Focused Direction To Go In!

KNOW WHAT YOU WANT – LIST YOUR TOP 10 GOALS

List the top 10 things you want to do in the next few years or even in your lifetime. Just jot down anything that comes to mind as being important to you that isn't currently a part of your life

Top 10 Goals:

1...
....

2...
....

3…………………………………………………………………………
…………………………………………………………………………..

4……………………………...……………………………………
………………………………………………………..……………

5………………………………………………………………………
……………………………………………………..………………

6………………………………………………………………………
………………………………………………...………………………

7……………………………………………...……………………
…………………………………………...……………………………..

8………………………………………….…………………………
……………………………….…………………………...……………

9……………………………………….…………………………
……………………………………………………...………..

10………….……………………………………...……………
………………………………………………………..…………

My Top 5 most important goals, in order, are:

1…….…………………..……..……………………………
…………………………………………..…..……………..

2……………………………..……..……………………………
……………………………..……………………………………

3...

....

4..

....

5..

....

And for what purpose? BE SPECIFIC!!!

This is very important: Why do you want to achieve these goals, why are they important to you. If you cannot give answers to these, then maybe you need to reconsider if they are that important! Are these goals aligned with your true purpose, and are you prepared to spend your time, energy and money on these goals.

Goal 1:

....

....

....

....

....

Goal 2:

....

....

....

....

....

Goal 3:

....
....
....
....
....

Goal 4:

....
....
....
....
....

Goal 5:

....
....
....
....
....

NOTES:...

....
....
....
....
....
....
....

. . . .
. . . .
. . . .
. . . .

MARRYING YOUR TOP 5 PRIORITIES

You must be sure you're committed to your Top 5 over everything else you do.

Ask yourself "Do I have a 'true desire' to achieve the goals, and why is this goal more important than anything in the world?"

Do this for your Top 5 below. Do you care about your Top 5 enough to not let anything get in the way?

Top 5:

1. . . . .
. . . .

2. . . . .
. . . .

3. . . . .
. . . .

4. . . . .
. . . .

5. . . . .
. . . .

Why are they more important than anything else in the world:

1...
....
....
....

2...
....
....
....

3...
....
....
....

4...
....
....
....

5...
....
....
....

Now that you have done this exercise you can outlay the rest of your **plan of action** using the two very effective formulas called the Ultimate Success Formula and SMART Goals.

The Ultimate Success Formula

How to use the Ultimate Success Formula:

1. **What is your goal/outcome?** Firstly identify what your goal is and what outcome you want from it!

2. **Why is achieving this goal important?** You need to ask yourself "Why is this the most important thing I need to do right now?" If you cannot give yourself a clear answer, then maybe you need to ask yourself "Is this the goal I really want to achieve right now?"

3. **How confident are you from 1–100% that you can achieve this goal?** If you are not 100% confident you can achieve this goal, then relook to see if this goal is too big right now. Make another one that leads up to that goal.

4. **What would need to happen for you to be 100% confident?** You will need to brain-storm here to see what you need to do, learn, research etc for you to be confident that you can complete this goal. You don't want to be wasting time, money and effort into something that you will not complete.

5. **What do you need to do to achieve this goal?** This is where you need to identify **all the steps** you need to take, what resources you need to gather etc to succeed in completing this goal.

6. **Prioritize them with no. 1 being the highest level of importance.** Once you have identified all the steps you need to take, put them into order of importance, starting with the most important step and then the next and so forth.

7. **Take the TOP 3 priorities and break them down further.** The more information you write down, the clearer you can become in what you need to do.

8. **Take Action.** Now that everything is written down, and you have an order in which to do things, it is just a case of doing them step by step.

Success or Feedback. Keep taking the steps until your reach your goal. If no success is gained, then look at the experience as feedback, not failure. Know that you need to go back and look at the process and steps and see what you need to change or adjust.

9. **Evaluate.** If you don't have success, then take the feedback to number 5 and ask yourself "What do I need to do to achieve this goal?

"This formula is a very effective and powerful tool to use to help you get from where you are now, to where you want to be!"

Ultimate Success Formula

1. What is your goal / outcome?

2. Why is achieving this goal important?

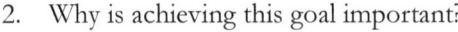

3. How confident are you from 1–100% that you can achieve this goal?

4. What would need to happen for you to be 100% confident?

5. What do you need to do to achieve this goal?

6. Prioritize them with no. 1 being the highest level of importance.

7. Take the TOP 3 priorities and break them down further.

8. Take Action

Success   Feedback

THERE IS NO FAILURE, ONLY FEEDBACK!

9. Evaluate – If you don't have success, then take the feedback to number 5 and ask yourself "What do I need to do to achieve this goal?

Ultimate Success Formula

On a scale of 1-10: "How much do you want to achieve your goal?"

$$1 - 2 - 3 - 4 - 5 - 6 - 7 - 8 - 9 - 10$$

On a scale of 1-10: "How much effort are you willing to commit to it?"

$$1 - 2 - 3 - 4 - 5 - 6 - 7 - 8 - 9 - 10$$

"If you aim at nothing, you will hit it every time"

Author Unkown

Example of getting what you ask for!

You are sitting in a restaurant and a waiter asks you to place your order, and you say "Please bring me something to eat and drink!"

When they bring you something and you don't like it, are you going to complain?

OR

Is it not better to be specific in what you want, to save you time and unnecessary delays in getting something that you actually want?

Because what you order, is what you will get!

S.M.A.R.T GOALS

One of the most effective ways of setting goals is using the **S.M.A.R.T formula**, which encompasses all the vital elements needed to maximize your goal setting success.

S = Specific: Be specific and clear in what you want to accomplish with ALL the details.

M = Measurable: How will you know if progress is being made on achieving your goals?

A = Attainable: Is attaining this goal achievable and realistic with effort and commitment? Do I have the resources to achieve this goal? If not, how will I get them?

R = Relevant: Why is your goal important to you, and is it relevant in your life's purpose? Is it in life with your core values and beliefs?

T = Timely / Time Bound: When do you want to achieve this goal? Have a clearly defined starting time and deadline.

Once you have done your **S.M.A.R.T Goals**, you take that information and place it into the **Goals Action Plan Boxes** which will help you with **Tasks To Do**, and **Action Plan**, and will help **Identify Obstacles** and **Challenges** you may encounter, and what action you will take to overcome them!

S.M.A.R.T GOALS

Today's date ....

What is your goal? Take the most important one from your list you created!

What do you want to accomplish?

And very importantly, for what purpose? (Be very specific in your purpose)

....

....

....

....

....

....

....

....

....

....

....

....

....

....

....

....

....

....

S.M.A.R.T GOALS

Today's date ....

S = Specific:

Be specific and clear in what you want to accomplish with ALL the details

Action words – build - design – implement – sell -

.... ‾ .... ‾ .... ‾ ....

.... ‾ .... ‾ .... ‾ ....

 What is your goal, what do you want to accomplish and for what purpose?

....

....

....

....

....

....

....

....

....

....

....

....

....

....

S.M.A.R.T GOALS

Today's date ....

M = Measurable:

How will you know if progress is being made on achieving your goals?

How will you know when you have reached your goal?

....

....

....

....

....

....

....

....

....

....

....

....

....

....

....

....

....

S.M.A.R.T GOALS

Today's date ....

A = Attainable:

Is attaining this goal achievable and realistic with effort and commitment?

Do I have the resources to achieve this goal? If not, how will I get them?

....

....

....

....

....

....

....

....

....

....

....

....

....

....

....

....

....

....

S.M.A.R.T GOALS

Today's date ....

R = Relevant:

Why is your goal important to you, and is it relevant in your life's purpose?

Is it in life with your core values and beliefs?

....
....
....
....
....
....
....
....
....
....
....
....
....
....
....
....
....
....
....

S.M.A.R.T GOALS

Today's date ....

T = Timely / Time Bound:

When do you want to achieve this goal?

Have a clearly defined starting time and deadline.

....
....
....
....
....
....
....
....
....
....
....
....
....
....
....
....
....
....
....
....

S.M.A.R.T

GOALS ACTION PLAN

TASK / TO DO	COMPLETION DATE

S.M.A.R.T

GOALS ACTION PLAN OBSTACLES / CHALLENGES

What obstacles and challenges stand in your way of achieving your goal?

OBSTACLES	HOW WILL YOU ADDRESS THE CHALLENGES WHEN THEY ARISE?

MY GOAL ....

FOR WHAT PURPOSE? ....

....

WEEKS
MONTHS
YEARS
·················
TIME FRAME

What steps do I need to take to reach my goal from where I am now, to where I want to be?

Now go back to page 90 and do the Life's Satisfaction Scorecard again, and see what score you get this time. If you don't get 10 for each, then go back and see what specifically you have to do to get a score of 10 for each question!

"A successful man is one who can lay a firm foundation with the bricks others have thrown at him!"
– David Brinkley

8.
CONCLUSION

"Remember life is a series of self-created lessons. Am I learning?"
Allan Rufus

I trust this book has been a help to you, and will guide you to getting that perfect job you want.

Life is a growing experience, and as long as each one of us is open to all possibilities, then anything is possible. The more we do something, the better we become. So, prepare yourself as best as possible through the mind, then go out and do the action.

I wish you great success in all your endeavours and may you take the steps to fulfill the dreams you envision!

I would like to end this book with a powerful declaration that has worked for me and many people who have used it. The declaration is requesting for a most benevolent outcome for you. How it works:- Once you say your most benevolent outcome out loud, the universal forces can help you manifest your request. It is a very powerful technique to use, and can be used to help manifest any good and positive thing in your life, including a desired job, as long as it does not infringe on the will of another person.

Say out loud *"I request a Most Benevolent Outcome for the job that is most perfect for me and my Personal Growth to come to me now, and may it be better in all ways than what I could hope for or expect! Thank you!"*

"Life is like a game of chess.

To win you have to make a move, knowing which move to make comes with IN-SIGHT and knowledge, and by learning the lessons that are accumulated along the way!"
- Allan Rufus

"Every expert had to start at the beginning, and now it is your time!"

- Allan Rufus

OTHER <u>PERSONAL DEVELOPMENT</u> BOOKS WRITTEN BY ALLAN RUFUS

http://www.allanrufus.org

The Master's Sacred Knowledge

The Minds Use-Fullness Depends On The Thoughts Of The User.

Today…we are going to fly high.

ABOUT THE AUTHOR

Allan Rufus, Author, Speaker, Life Coach, NLP Coach in both Corporate and Personal Development, Time Line Therapy Coach, Trainer and TEFL Teacher has been training and developing individuals for over a decade inspiring them to achieve their best. His purpose is to transform people's lives to help them achieve their goals in which ever field they choose to adventure in.

Allan Rufus is Certified with AUNLP - American Union Of NLP. An Associate Certified NLP Coach, A Corporate & Personal Coach recognized by ACC – Associate Coach Federation and ICF – International Coach federation.

www.ingramcontent.com/pod-product-compliance
Lightning Source LLC
Chambersburg PA
CBHW051500170526
45166CB00001B/327